PRECALCULUS

CLEP* Test Study Guide

All rights reserved. This Study Guide, Book and Flashcards are protected under the US Copyright Law. No part of this book or study guide or flashcards may be reproduced, distributed or stored in a retrieval system, or transmitted in any form or by any means, electronic, mechanical, photocopying, recording, or otherwise, without the prior written permission of the publisher Breely Crush Publishing, LLC.

© 2026 Breely Crush Publishing, LLC

*CLEP is a registered trademark of the College Entrance Examination Board which does not endorse this book.

971010822143

Copyright ©2003 - 2026, Breely Crush Publishing, LLC.

All rights reserved.

This Study Guide, Book and Flashcards are protected under the US Copyright Law. No part of this publication may be reproduced, distributed or stored in a retrieval system, or transmitted in any form or by any means, electronic, mechanical, photocopying, recording, or otherwise, without the prior written permission of the publisher Breely Crush Publishing, LLC.

Published by Breely Crush Publishing, LLC
10808 River Front Parkway
South Jordan, UT 84095
www.breelycrushpublishing.com

ISBN-10: 1-61433-645-8
ISBN-13: 978-1-61433-645-7

Printed and bound in the United States of America.

CLEP is a registered trademark of the College Entrance Examination Board which does not endorse this book.

Table of Contents

Algebraic Expressions, Equations, and Inequalities *1*
Polynomials *2*
Distributive Property *4*
Quadratic Equations *6*
Radical Equations *7*
Logarithms *10*
Exponential Equations *11*
Systems *12*
Partial Fraction Decomposition *14*
Absolute Value *16*
Rational Functions *16*
Trigonometric Functions *17*
Algebraic Inequalities *19*
Functions and Their Graphs *20*
Representations of Functions:Symbolic, Graphical, and Tabular *23*
Analytical Geometry *35*
Parabola *36*
Ellipse *37*
Hyperbola *38*
Trigonometry and Its Applications *39*
Trigonometric Functions Based on the Unit Circle *41*
Formulas to Memorize *42*
Sample Test Questions *44*
Answer Key *97*
Special Information for the CLEP Test *98*
Test Taking Strategies *98*
What Your Score Means *99*
Test Preparation *99*
Legal Note *100*

 Algebraic Expressions, Equations, and Inequalities

What is an algebraic expression? Expressions contain numbers and variables that are called "terms". An algebraic expression does **NOT** have an equal sign. It is simply a collection of terms that are separated by arithmetic operations including addition, subtraction, multiplication, and division.

How do you combine algebraic expressions? There are three main steps involved in combining (or simplifying) an algebraic expression. The three steps include:

1. Identify "like" terms.
2. Add or subtract the coefficients of "like" terms.
3. Multiply the number found in Step 2 by the common variables(s).

In order to complete these three steps, you need to understand a few definitions:

"Like" terms: Two terms are considered "like" terms if they have the **SAME** variable with the **SAME** exponent. For example, $2x$ and $3x$ are like terms because they have the same variable "x" and this variable has the same exponent of 1.

Coefficient of the Variable: The coefficient of the variable is the number that is multiplied by the variable. In other words, the coefficient of the variable is the number directly in front of the variable. For example, the coefficient of $3x$ is 3 and the coefficient of $0.75y$ is 0.75.

The coefficient of the variable is sometimes referred to as the "Numerical Coefficient" and it can be positive, negative, an Integer, fraction, or decimal.

Examples of Combining Algebraic Expressions:

1.) $2x + 3x$ Answer: $5x$

2.) $10y + 9 + 14y - 5$ Answer: $24y + 4$

3.) $3x^2 + 2x - 5x^2 + 6y$ Answer: $-2x^2 + 2x + 6y$

Polynomials

What are Polynomials? A polynomial is an expression containing the sum of a finite number of terms of the form ax^n, for any real number a and any whole number n.

Examples of Polynomials:

$x^2 + 6x + 5$

$2x^3 + 3x^2 + 4x + 16$

How do you ADD and SUBTRACT two polynomials?
There are two general steps you take to add and subtract polynomials. The two steps include:

Step #1: Remove parentheses

Step #2: Combine "like" terms

Question: Evaluate $(x^2 + 8x + 12) + (2x^2 - 3x + 13)$
This is an ADDITION problem.

1.) Remove the parentheses

Note: There is a positive 1 on the outside of each parenthesis.

Therefore, you multiply a positive 1 by each term to remove the parentheses.

$1(x^2 + 8x + 12) + 1(2x^2 - 3x + 13)$

$x^2 + 8x + 12 + 2x^2 - 3x + 13$

2.) Combine "like" terms

$x^2 + 2x^2 + 8x - 3x + 12 + 13$

Answer: $3x^2 + 5x + 25$

Question: Evaluate $(x^2 + 8x + 12) - (2x^2 - 3x + 13)$

This is a SUBTRACTION problem.

1.) Remove the parentheses

   Note: There is a positive one by the first set of parentheses, but a NEGATIVE one by the second set of parentheses because you are dealing with subtraction. The signs of the first polynomial remain the same and change the signs of the second polynomial to their opposites.

   $(x^2 + 8x + 12) - (2x^2 - 3x + 13)$

   $1(x^2 + 8x + 12) - 1(2x^2 - 3x + 13)$

   $x^2 + 8x + 12 - 2x^2 + 3x - 13$

2.) Combine "like" terms

   $x^2 - 2x^2 + 8x + 3x + 12 - 13$

   Answer: $-x^2 + 11x - 1$

How do I multiply two terms that have variables with exponents?

You will need to know the "Rules of Exponents" to multiply two terms that have variables with exponents. To use these rules you **MUST** have the **SAME** Variable.

Basic rules of exponents

Product Rule: When multiplying two terms, just **ADD** their exponents and **MULTIPLY** their coefficients.

   Question:

   $2x^3 \times 3x^4$

   $(2 \times 3)(x^3 \times x^4)$

   Answer: $6x^7$

Quotient Rule: When dividing two terms, just **SUBTRACT** their exponents and **DIVIDE** their coefficients. Note: You MUST subtract the bottom exponent from the top exponent.

Question: $\dfrac{6x^{10}}{3x^2}$

Answer: $2x^8$

Power Rule: Use this rule when a term is inside parentheses AND raised to a power. In this case you would **MULTIPLY** the exponents and coefficients by the power on the outside of the parentheses.

Question:
$(2x^5)^3$
$(2)^3(x^5)^3$

Answer: $8x^{15}$

How do you MULTIPLY AND DIVIDE two polynomials?

Two types of multiplication include:
- Multiplication using the Distributive property.
- Multiplication of two binomials using the FOIL method.

Distributive Property

How to multiply terms using the Distributive Property:

Evaluate: $2x(x + 14)$

Multiply the term "$2x$" by **EACH** term on the inside of the parentheses.

Question:
$2x(x+14)$
$2x(x)+2x(14)$

Answer: $2x^2 + 28x$

How do you multiply two binomials using the "FOIL" method?
Use the FOIL method to multiply two binomials.

Question: Evaluate $(x + 3)(x + 4)$

Multiply **F**IRST Terms: $(\mathbf{x} + 3)(\mathbf{x} + 4) = x^2$

Multiply **O**uter Terms: $(\mathbf{x} + 3)(x + \mathbf{4}) = 4x$

Multiply **I**nner Terms: $(x + \mathbf{3})(\mathbf{x} + 4) = 3x$

Multiply **L**ast Terms: $(x + \mathbf{3})(x + \mathbf{4}) = 12$

Therefore, $x^2 + 4x + 3x + 12$

Combine "like" terms:

Answer: $x^2 + 7x + 12$

What is an algebraic equation? Equations contain numbers and variables that are called "terms". An algebraic equation must have an equal sign. Equations must always be in "balance" meaning that the value of each side of the equation is the same.

How do you solve a Linear equation? You need to follow specific procedures when solving an equation. The two main goals you need to accomplish include moving the variable to one side of the equal sign and setting the coefficient of the variable equal to 1.

Example of a "One" Step Linear Equation: Solve $x + 10 = 28$

The variable "x" already has a coefficient of 1 so we need to move 10 to the other side of the equation. Therefore, you will add the opposite of 10 to each side of the equation. Remember: When you complete an operation on one side of the equation you MUST do the exact same operation to the other side of the equation.

$$x + 10 = 28$$
$$x + (10 - 10) = (28 - 10)$$
$$x + 0 = 18$$
$$x = 18$$

Example of a "Two" Step Linear Equation: Solve $2x + 15 = 45$

First, move 15 to the other side of the equation so that $2x$ is by itself on one side.

$$2x + 15 = 45$$
$$2x + (15 - 15) = (45 - 15)$$
$$2x = 30$$

The second step is to make the coefficient of the variable 1. Therefore, divide each side by 2.

$$2x = 30$$
$$\frac{2x}{2} = \frac{30}{2} = 15$$

Therefore, $x = 15$

Note: Dividing by 2 is the equivalent to multiplying its reciprocal of ½.

Example of "Two" Step Linear Equation using a Reciprocal: Solve $\frac{2}{3}x + 2 = 8$

$$\frac{2}{3}x + 2 = 8$$
$$\frac{2}{3}x + (2 - 2) = (8 - 2)$$
$$\frac{2}{3}x = 6$$
$$\frac{3}{2} * \frac{2}{3}x = 6 * \frac{3}{2}$$
$$x = 9$$

Quadratic Equations

What is a quadratic equation? A quadratic equation in one variable is an equation that can be changed into the form $ax^2 + bx + c = 0$, where a, b, and c are real constants. A **solution** to a quadratic equation is always a **root** of the polynomial $ax^2 + bx + c = 0$.

How do you find the "root" of a polynomial? The roots of a polynomial can be found by **factoring** the polynomial. Set each factor equal to "0" and solve the equation.

Question: Find the solutions to the Quadratic equation: $x^2 + 7x + 12$

Factor to find: $(x + 3)(x + 4)$

$x + 3 = 0$ Therefore $x = -3$

$x + 4 = 0$ Therefore $x = -4$

The solutions are -3 and -4.

How do you solve a quadratic equation using the "square root" property? The square root property says that if you set $x^2 = a$ then $x = \pm\sqrt{a}$.

Question: Solve $x^2 = 36$

Answer: $x = \pm\sqrt{36} = \pm 6$

How do you solve a quadratic equation by using the quadratic formula?
Follow these two steps:

1. Write the equation in standard form, $ax^2 + bx + c = 0$, and determine the numerical values for a, b, and c.

2. Substitute the values for a, b, and c from Step 1 in the quadratic formula below and then evaluate to obtain the solution.

<u>**THE QUADRATIC FORMULA:**</u>

$$x = \frac{-b \pm \sqrt{b^2 - 4ac}}{2a}$$

Radical Equations

What is a radical equation? A "radical" is essentially a square root, except that radical is the overarching term which can describe any type of "root"; i.e., square roots $\sqrt{}$, cube roots $\sqrt[3]{}$, fourth roots $\sqrt[4]{}$, and so on. A radical equation, therefore, is any equation that has a radical in it. Note: an expression is only a radical equation if the x-variable is inside the square root. √x+2 IS a radical expression. √2+x IS NOT a radical expression.

How do you solve radical equations? Radical equations are closely related to polynomial and quadratic equations because the two are opposite operations. In other words, a radical "undoes" an exponent. Therefore, exponents can be used in solving radical equations. For example:

Solve $\sqrt[4]{x+2} = 2$

$$\sqrt[4]{x+2} = 2$$
$$\sqrt[4]{x+2}^4 = 2^4$$
$$x + 2 = 16$$
$$x = 14$$

Solving radical equations may seem fairly straightforward, but there are a couple of tips to be aware of to help you avoid making mistakes.

<u>Tip #1</u>: Be aware of extraneous solutions. Extraneous solutions are solutions that emerge as mathematically correct, but which are actually false or irrelevant to the question at hand. These often emerge when working with radicals and exponents because of the "±" which you put in front of a square root. It creates an extra answer that won't actually work in the original equation. The following example will demonstrate this.

Solve $\sqrt{x-1} = x - 7$

The two functions represented by this equation are $y = x - 7$ and $\sqrt{x-1}$ and graph as:

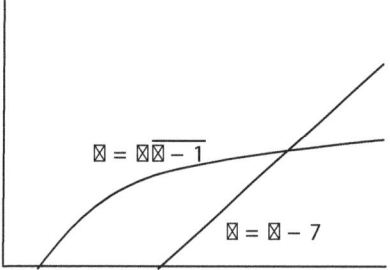

As you can see the graph has a single intersection point. Moving back to the original equation, we can proceed to solve it algebraically.

$$\sqrt{x-1} = x - 7$$
$$\sqrt{x-1}^2 = (x-7)^2$$
$$x - 1 = x^2 - 14x + 49$$
$$0 = x^2 - 15x + 50$$
$$0 = (x-5)(x-10)$$
$$x = 5, 10$$

The algebraic method provided two solutions, when we know that only one exists based on the graph. We can conclude, therefore, that one of the results must be extraneous. This is why it is important that whenever you finish solving an equation, you plug both numbers back into your original equation and ensure that they are, in fact, true.

X=5, FALSE
$$\sqrt{(5)-1} = (5) - 7$$
$$\sqrt{4} = -2$$
$$2 = -2$$

X=10, TRUE
$$\sqrt{10-1} = 10 - 7$$
$$\sqrt{9} = 3$$
$$3 = 3$$

Therefore $x = 10$ is the only correct solution to the equation.

Tip #2: Use common sense. Many times people will overlook that there is not a solution to a radical expression and solve for an incorrect solution. Remember, an even exponent will NEVER yield a negative result. Some examples of this follow:

$\sqrt{x} = -2$ yields the solution $x = 4$, which is extraneous.

However,

$\sqrt[3]{x} = -1$ yields the solution $x = -1$ which IS possible because ODD roots CAN yield negative answers.

Tip #3: Make sure that you deal with SIDES when solving equations and not individual TERMS. The following example illustrates the difference between these two.

Solve $\sqrt{x+5} - 1 = 4$

Incorrect solution:

$$\sqrt{x+5}^2 - 1^2 = 4^2$$
$$x + 5 - 1 = 16$$

Correct solution:

$$(\sqrt{x+5} - 1)^2 = 4^2$$
$$(x+5) - 2\sqrt{x+5} + 1 = 16$$

Clearly these two methods will yield different solutions to the equation.

Tip #4: Whenever possible, get the radical ALONE before raising to an exponent. Otherwise the equation may simply become more complex or yield false answers as a result. This is true in the case of the above equation, and is further illustrated below.

Solve $\sqrt{x+5} - 1 = 4$

Simpler way:

$\sqrt{x+5} - 1 = 4$
$\sqrt{x+5} = 5$
$\sqrt{x+5}^2 = 5^2$
$x + 5 = 25$
$x = 20$

Harder way:

$(\sqrt{x+5} - 1)^2 = 4^2$
$(x+5) - 2\sqrt{x+5} + 1 = 16$
$x - 10 = 2\sqrt{x+5}$
$x^2 - 20x - 100 = 4(x+5)$
$x^2 - 20x - 100 = 4x + 20$
...etc.

 Logarithms

What are logarithms? Logarithms represent the exponent of a positive number. For example, if $b^x = N$ where "N" is a positive number and "b" is a positive number besides 1, then the exponent "x" is the logarithm of N to the base b.

This relationship can be written as $x = \log_b N$

Following are examples that will help demonstrate this relationship:

Example 1: Write $4^2 = 16$ using logarithmic notation.
2 is the logarithm of 16 to the base 4 therefore logarithmic notation is $2 = \log_4 16$

Example 2: Evaluate $\log_4 64$.
$\log_4 64$ says that you have a base = 4 and you have to figure out what x value to use in order to satisfy $4^x = 64$. Therefore, $x = 3$ and $\log_4 64 = 3$.

LAWS OF LOGARITHMS: There are 3 basic laws of logarithms which include:

1. The logarithm of the product of two positive numbers M and N is equal to the sum of the logarithms of the numbers

   $\log_b MN = \log_b M + \log_b N$

   For example, $\log_2 3(5) = \log_2 3 + \log_2 5$

2. The logarithm of the quotient of two positive numbers M and N is equal to the difference of the logarithms of the numbers

   $\log_b \frac{M}{N} = \log_b M - \log_b N$

For example, $\log_{10}\dfrac{17}{24} = \log_{10} 17 - \log_{10} 24$

3. The logarithm of the "p^{th}" power of a positive number M is equal to "p" multiplied by the logarithm of the number $\log_b M^p = p\log_b M$.

   For example, $\log_8 6^4 = 4\log_8 6$

What are Natural Logarithms? Natural logarithms have a base "e" which is a constant. Natural logarithms are denoted by *ln*.

You can find "e" on your scientific calculator. $e = 2.718281828\ldots$
$ln a = b$ is $e^b = a$

When would you use logarithms and exponents? Logarithms and exponents can be used when you calculate simple & compound interest and exponential growth.

Exponential Equations

What is an exponential equation? Exponential equations are closely linked to logarithmic equations because the two are opposite operations. An exponential equation appears in the form $y = b^x$, so that the "x" variable is the exponent that must be solved for and "b" is some constant base.

How are exponential equations solved? Exponential equations can be solved using logarithms. Remember that logarithmic equations and exponential equations are inverses such that $\log_b b^x = x$. Similarly, the reverse is also true ($b^{\log_b x} = x$).

Example #1: Solve $2e^{4x} = 10$

This is an exponential equation, so we must use logarithms to isolate the x and get it out of the exponent. The solution is:

$2e^{4x} = 10$
$e^{4x} = 5$
$4x = \ln 5$
$x = \dfrac{\ln 5}{4}$

Example #2: Solve $\log_4(3x + 1) = 2$

This is a logarithmic equation so we must use exponents to isolate the x and get it out of the log. This is done by raising both sides to the exponent "4" which will cancel the logarithm. The solution is:

$$\log_4(3x + 1) = 2$$
$$4^{\log_4(3x+1)} = 4^2$$
$$3x + 1 = 16$$
$$x = 5$$

How do you deal with inequalities in logarithms and exponential equations? When an inequality appears in an exponential equation or logarithmic equation, treat it the same as you would any other type of inequality. Simply solve for x and, if necessary, graph the inequality and shade the appropriate areas.

Systems

What are systems of Linear Equations? Systems of equations contain more than one equation. Solutions to a system of equations satisfy ALL the equations.

How do you find solutions to a system of Linear Equations?
Solve systems of linear equations by using the "Addition Method".
Follow these six steps:

1. If necessary, rewrite each equation so that the terms containing variables appear on the left hand side of the equal sign and any constants appear on the right side of the equal sign.

2. If necessary, multiply one or both equations by a constant(s) so that when the equations are added the resulting sum will contain only one variable.

3. Add the equations. This will yield a single equation containing only one variable.

4. Solve for the variable in the equation from step 3.

5. a) Substitute the value found in step 4 into either of the original equations. Solve that equation to find the value of the remaining variable.

OR

b) Repeat steps 2-4 to eliminate the other variable.

6. Check the values obtained in all original equations.

    Question: Solve $x + 3y = 13$ (Equation 1)

    $x + 4y = 18$ (Equation 2)

    Multiply Equation 1 by -1.
    $$-1(x + 3y) = -1(13) \rightarrow -x - 3y = -13$$

    Add Equation 1 and Equation 2
    $$-x - 3y = -13$$
    $$x + 4y = 18$$
    $$y = 5$$

    Plug $y = 5$ into the original Equation 1 to find $x = -2$. Check that this solution satisfies both equations.

What are systems of nonlinear equations? Nonlinear systems of equations are sets of equations just like linear systems of equations, however they require you to use more complex operations. In some cases this may include radicals, trigonometric ratios, absolute values, logarithms, or exponents. However, while the specific operations involved may be more complex, nonlinear equations and inequalities are treated the same as linear systems. Simply solve for x and/or graph as necessary.

Example of solving a nonlinear system of equations: Find the solution of the following system of equations:

$$y = x^2 + 2x + 1$$
$$y = 2x^2 - 2$$

To solve the system of equations, simply set the two equations equal to each other and solve for x.

$$x^2 + 2x + 1 = 2x^2 - 2$$
$$0 = x^2 - 2x - 3$$
$$0 = (x + 1)(x - 3)$$
$$x = -1, 3$$

Therefore, the graphs intersect in two places. Both at $x = -1$ and $x = 3$. We can find the exact point at which they insect by plugging these values back into either of the original equations.

$$x = -1; y = 2(-1)^2 - 2 = 0$$
$$x = 3; y = 2(3)^2 - 2 = 15$$

So solution to the system of equations is the points (-1,0) and (3, 15).

 Partial Fraction Decomposition

What is partial fraction decomposition? One skill which can be very useful in simplifying mathematic operations is partial fraction decomposition. In previous math classes you should have learned how to add together a series of fractions which have different denominators, to create one larger fraction. Partial Fraction Decomposition involves doing just the opposite.

How is partial fraction decomposition done? With partial fraction decomposition the goal is to break a larger, more complex equation into smaller, manageable parts. To do this, follow the following series of steps.

1. Completely factor the denominator of the expression.
2. Set the expression equal to a series of added fractions, each with one factor of the denominator as their denominator.
3. Multiply all terms by the total denominator.
4. Solve for the numerators of the broken down fractions by plugging in values of x.

Example: Use partial fraction decomposition to break down the following fraction

$$\frac{3x+1}{x^2+5x-14}$$

Step 1: Completely factor the denominator

$$\frac{3x+1}{x^2+5x-14} = \frac{3x+1}{(x+7)(x-2)}$$

Step 2: Set the expression equal to a series of added fractions, each with one factor of the denominator as their denominator

$$\frac{3x+1}{(x+7)(x-2)} = \frac{A}{(x+7)} + \frac{B}{(x-2)}$$

Note: A and B represent the numerators which must still be solved for. If there were additional expressions in the overall denominator, we would have addition expressions ranging from C to D to E as necessary.

Step 3: Multiply all terms by the total denominator

$$\frac{3x+1}{(x+7)(x-2)} = \frac{A}{(x+7)} + \frac{B}{(x-2)}$$

$$\frac{3x+1}{(x+7)(x-2)}(x+7)(x-2) = \frac{A}{(x+7)}(x+7)(x-2) + \frac{B}{(x-2)})(x+7)(x-2)$$

$$3x+1 = A(x-2) + B(x+7)$$

Step 4: Solve for the numerators of the broken down fractions by plugging in values of x. Choose values of x that will eliminate one of the variables (either A or B). In this case we will use $x = 2$ and $x = -7$.

Using x=2:

$$3x+1 = A(x-2) + B(x+7)$$
$$3(2)+1 = A(2-2) + B(2+7)$$
$$7 = 9B$$
$$B = \frac{7}{9}$$

Using x=-7

$$3x+1 = A(x-2) + B(x+7)$$
$$3(-7)+1 = A(-7-2) + B(-7+7)$$
$$-20 = -9A$$
$$A = \frac{20}{9}$$

Therefore, the partial fraction decomposition of $\frac{3x+1}{x^2+5x-14}$ is:

$$\frac{20}{9(x+7)} + \frac{7}{9(x-2)}$$

What can make partial fraction decomposition more complex: The more complex the denominator involved is, the more complex the partial fraction decomposition will be. This is because there will both be additional numerators to solve for, and these numerators become more complex. If a denominator factors to have a squared term, this term will have an "$Ax + B$" as the numerator, rather than simply an "A." The following are examples of the breakdowns of some more complex decompositions.

$$\frac{7x}{(x^2+3)(x+1)} = \frac{Ax+B}{x^2+3} + \frac{C}{x+1}$$

$$\frac{x+1}{(x-1)^2(3x-1)} = \frac{A}{(x-1)} + \frac{Bx+C}{(x-1)^2} + \frac{D}{3x-1}$$

$$\frac{x^2+2x+1}{(x+7)^2(2x+1)(x-2)} = \frac{A}{x+7} + \frac{Bx+C}{(x+7)^2} + \frac{D}{(2x+1)} + \frac{E}{(x-2)}$$

Absolute Value

What is absolute value? Absolute value refers to the distance between a number and 0 on the number line. Absolute value is always positive.

What is the notation for Absolute Value and how do we find it?
The notation for absolute value is $|\ |$.
You change the sign of the number inside the $|\ |$ to a positive number.

Examples of Absolute Value:

$$|-2| = 2 \qquad |4| = 4 \qquad \left|\frac{-3}{4}\right| = \frac{3}{4}$$

Note: $-|-2| = -2$

Question: Find the solutions for $|3x - 5| = 2x$.
  If $2x \geq 0$ then $3x - 5 = 2x$ where $x = 5$
  OR $3x - 5 = -2x$ where $x = 1$.

Rational Functions

What are "Rational" functions? A rational function is the ratio between two polynomial functions. If $P(x)$ and $Q(x)$ are polynomials then a function of the form $R(x) = P(x) \div Q(x)$ is a rational function where $Q(x) \neq 0$.

NOTE: Rational functions have "vertical" and "horizontal" asymptotes.

Vertical Asymptotes are the values of x that make $Q(x) = 0$ if $P(x) \neq 0$.

For example, find the vertical asymptotes of $R(x) = \dfrac{2x - 3}{x^2 - 4}$

$R(x)$ is undefined where $x^2 - 4 = 0$, so $x = 2$ and $x = -2$ could result in vertical asymptotes. Next you have to make sure that when $x = 2$ and $x = -2$ that $R(x) \neq 0$. Plug in the values for x and the $R(x) \neq 0$ so $x = 2$ and $x = -2$ are in fact vertical asymptotes.

Horizontal Asymptotes occur at $y = a$ if, as $|x|$ increases without limit, $R(x)$ approaches a. $R(x)$ has at most one horizontal asymptote. You can find the horizontal asymptote of $R(x)$ by comparing the degree of $P(x)$ to the degree of $Q(x)$.

1) If the degree of $P(x)$ < degree of $Q(x)$ then $R(x)$ has a horizontal asymptote of $y = 0$.

2) If the degree of $P(x)$ = degree of $Q(x)$ then $R(x)$ has a horizontal asymptote of $y = \dfrac{a_n}{b_n}$ where a_n is the coefficient with the highest degree term of $P(x)$ and b_n is the coefficient with the highest degree term of $Q(x)$.

3) If the degree of $P(x)$ > degree of $Q(x)$ then $R(x)$ does **NOT** have a horizontal asymptote.

   Example, what are the horizontal asymptotes of the following Rational Function?

   $$R(x) = \dfrac{2x+1}{3+5x}$$

   Answer: The numerator and denominator both have a degree of 1. The highest coefficient of $P(x)$ is 2 and the highest coefficient of $Q(x)$ is 5 then $R(x)$ has a horizontal asymptote of $y = 2/5$.

 Trigonometric Functions

What are trigonometric functions? Trigonometric functions are functions that include the trigonometric ratios. You should be familiar with six different trigonometric ratios: sine, cosine, tangent, secant, cosecant and cotangent.

$$sinx = \dfrac{opp}{hyp} \quad cosx = \dfrac{adj}{hyp} \quad tanx = \dfrac{opp}{adj} \quad secx = \dfrac{1}{cosx} \quad cscx = \dfrac{1}{sinx} \quad cotx = \dfrac{1}{tanx}$$

How to solve trigonometric functions: Solving trigonometric equations is simple if you have a firm grasp of the different ratios. The following table lists the various ratios and equations that you should be familiar with in order to manipulate trigonometric functions.

Pythagorean Identities	Even/Odd Identities
$\sin^2\theta + \cos^2\theta = 1$	$\sin(-x) = -\sin x$
$\tan^2\theta + 1 = \sec^2\theta$	$\cos(-x) = \cos(x)$
$1 + \cot^2\theta = \csc^2\theta$	$\tan(-x) = -\tan(x)$
Co-function Identities	**Reciprocal Identities**
$\cos\left(\frac{\pi}{2} - x\right) = \sin x$	$\csc x = \frac{1}{\sin x}$
$\sin\left(\frac{\pi}{2} - x\right) = \cos x$	$\sec x = \frac{1}{\cos x}$
$\tan\left(\frac{\pi}{2} - x\right) = \cot x$	$\cot x = \frac{1}{\tan x}$
$\csc\left(\frac{\pi}{2} - x\right) = \sec x$	**Sum and Difference Formulas**
$\sec\left(\frac{\pi}{2} - x\right) = \csc x$	$\sin(x \pm y) = \sin x \cos y \pm \cos x \sin y$
Half-Angle Formulas	$\cos(x \pm y) = \cos x \cos y \mp \sin x \sin y$
$\sin\left(\frac{x}{2}\right) = \pm\sqrt{\frac{1 - \cos x}{2}}$	$\tan(x \pm y) = \frac{\tan x \pm \tan y}{1 \mp \tan x \tan y}$
$\cos\left(\frac{x}{2}\right) = \pm\sqrt{\frac{1 + \cos x}{2}}$	**Sum-to-Product Formulas**
$\tan\left(\frac{x}{2}\right) = \pm\frac{1 - \cos x}{\sin x}$	$\sin x \pm \sin y = 2\sin\left(\frac{x \pm y}{2}\right)\cos\left(\frac{x \mp y}{2}\right)$
Double Angle Formulas	$\cos x + \cos y = 2\cos\left(\frac{x + y}{2}\right)\cos\left(\frac{x - y}{2}\right)$
$\sin 2\theta = 2\sin\theta\cos\theta$	$\cos x \cos y = -2\sin\left(\frac{x + y}{2}\right)\sin\left(\frac{x - y}{2}\right)$
$\cos 2\theta = \cos^2\theta - \sin^2\theta = 1 - 2\sin^2\theta$ $= 2\cos^2\theta - 1$	**Product-to-Sum Formulas**
$\tan 2\theta = \frac{2\tan\theta}{1 - \tan^2\theta}$	$\sin x \cdot \sin y = \frac{1}{2}[\cos(x - y) - \cos(x + y)]$
Law of Sines	$\cos x \cdot \cos y = \frac{1}{2}[\cos(x - y) + \cos(x + y)]$
$\frac{a}{\sin A} = \frac{b}{\sin B} = \frac{c}{\sin C}$	$\sin x \cdot \cos y = \frac{1}{2}[\sin(x + y) + \sin(x - y)]$
Law of Cosines	$\cos x \cdot \sin y = \frac{1}{2}[\sin(x + y) - \sin(x - y)]$
$a^2 = b^2 + c^2 - 2bc\cos A$	
$A = \cos^{-1}\left(\frac{b^2 + c^2 - a^2}{2bc}\right)$	

In addition to these ratios, you should also be familiar with a few basic values associated with the sine, cosine, and tangent functions. You should have the following memorized:

	sin(x)	cos(x)	tan(x)
$0 \, rad, 0°$	0	1	0
$\frac{\pi}{6}, 30°$	$\frac{1}{2}$	$\frac{\sqrt{3}}{2}$	$\frac{1}{\sqrt{3}}$
$\frac{\pi}{4}, 45°$	$\frac{\sqrt{2}}{2}$	$\frac{\sqrt{2}}{2}$	1
$\frac{\pi}{3}, 60°$	$\frac{\sqrt{3}}{2}$	$\frac{1}{2}$	$\sqrt{3}$
$\frac{\pi}{2}, 90°$	1	0	undefined

Algebraic Inequalities

What are the four equality signs? Read the following signs from left to right.

< is "less than"
\> is "greater than"
≤ is "less than or equal to"
≥ is "greater than or equal to"

You can use inequality signs in an algebraic equation format.

How do you solve Linear Inequalities in ONE variable?

Linear Inequality Example: Solve $x + 10 < 5$

Solve this as you would an equation keeping the < sign intact.

$$x + 10 < 5$$
$$x + (10 - 10) < (5 - 10)$$
$$x < -5$$

Linear Inequality Example: Solve $2x + 4 \geq 10$

$$2x + 4 \geq 10$$
$$2x + (4 - 4) \geq (10 - 4)$$
$$2x \geq 6$$
$$\frac{2x}{2} \geq \frac{6}{2}$$
$$x \geq 3$$

Special Rule when solving Inequalities: There is one special rule that you need to use when you have a $-x$ value to begin with. Remember that we want x to be positive and have a coefficient of 1. In the very last step of the inequality you divide each side of the inequality by a negative number. This means that you need to change the direction of the inequality sign to the opposite direction. This is ONLY when dividing (or multiplying by a reciprocal) by a NEGATIVE number.

Special Rule Linear Inequality Example: Solve and graph $-2x < 10$.

$$-2x < 10$$
$$\frac{-2x}{-2} < \frac{10}{-2}$$
$$x > -5$$

Functions and Their Graphs

What is a function? A mathematical function represents a systematic manner in which to find a *value*. In other words, when you input information into a function you will generate a specific "unique" output. A function is usually written as $f(x)$.

For example, let's look at the function: $f(x) = x + 2$ and the value of $x = 3$

The Input is the value $x = 3$ while the output will be what you find when you plug "3" in for x in the equation $f(x) = x + 2$.

$$f(x) = x + 2$$
$$f(3) = 3 + 2$$

Therefore, $f(3) = 5$

Can you figure out what the value of $f(10)$ given $f(x) = x + 2$?

$f(x) = x + 2$
$f(10) = 10 + 2$
Therefore, $f(10) = 12$

How do functions relate to graphing? Functions pair up x values with y values. Functions must have only one y (or output) value for each x (or input).

What is the domain of a function? The domain of a function refers to all the possible values you can use for "x" in the function $f(x)$ otherwise known as the first number in each ordered pair. The function $f(x) = 2x$ produced the following ordered pairs: (-1, -2), (0,0), (1,2), (2,4), (3,6). The Domain represents the numbers {-1, 0, 1, 2, and 3}.

What is the range of a function? The range of a function refers to all the possible values you can determine for the output $f(x)$ or "y". The range from the previous $f(x) = 2x$ is the second number in each ordered pair. (-1, -2), (0,0), (1,2), (2,4), (3,6). Therefore, the range is {-2, 0, 2, 4, 6}.

How can you tell if a graph represents a function? Use the "vertical line test" to determine if a graph represents a function. The vertical line test states that if you draw a vertical line through a piece of the graph and it intersects the graph at one more than one point then it is NOT a function. (Remember for every "x" value you can have only ONE "y" value in order for the relationship to be a function.)

Following is a visual representation to explain the vertical line test.

$f(x) = x^2$ is a function as the red vertical line passes through the graph at only one y value.

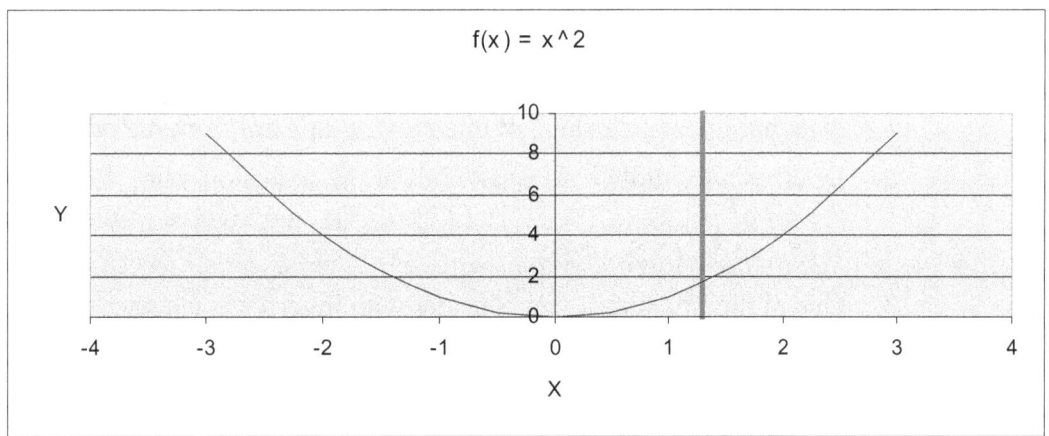

The following graph is NOT a function because the red vertical line passes through more then one *y* value.

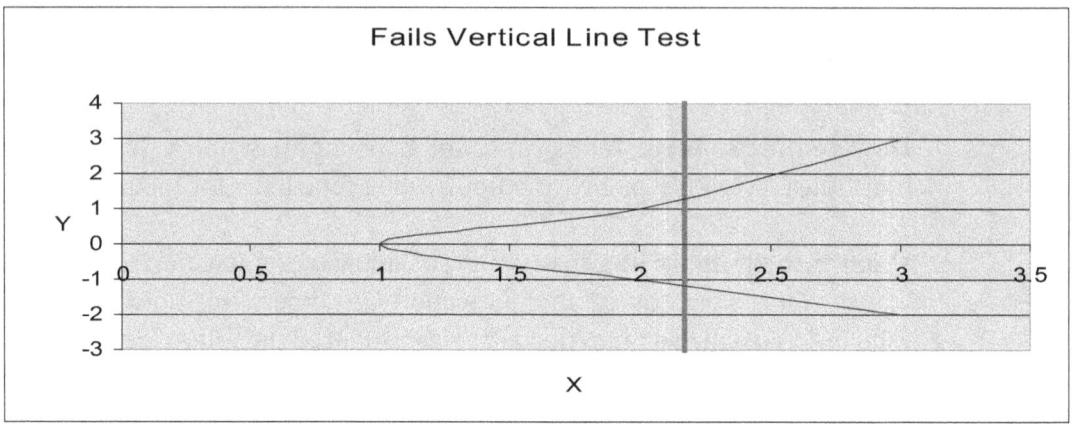

How do you find the Composition of two functions? The composition of two functions takes the terms of one function and substitutes them into the other function. The composition of two functions is denoted as $f(g(x))$.

For example, find $f(g(x))$

When $f(x) = x^2 + 10$ and $g(x) = 3x$

$f(g(x)) = f(3x) = (3x)^2 + 10 = 9x^2 + 10$

Therefore, $f(g(x)) = 9x^2 + 10$

How do you find the Inverse of a function? The inverse of a function can be found by switching the x variable with the y variable. For example, let $y = f(x) = x^2$ then the inverse is denoted as f^{-1} is $f^{-1}(x) = f(y) = y^2$.

Some other things to know about inverses:

1. The inverse of a function is that function reflected over the line $y = x$ (which is a diagonal line with a slope of one moving upward from the origin).

2. Inverses are simply a reversal of all of the points on a line. For instance, if given the set of points {(0,1), (1,4), (2,2), (3,4)}, the inverse would contain the points {(1,0), (4,1), (2,2), (4,3)}.

3. One of the first things you consider with inverses is whether or not the inverse of a function is also a function. In the example given above you can clearly see that this is not the case because the input of "4" would yield both "1" and "3".

4. You can discover whether the inverse of a function is also a function WITHOUT graphing it by using the "horizontal line test." This is the same as the vertical line test for functions, but uses horizontal lines and tells about inverses.
5. To solve for the inverse of a function, simply switch around the x's and y's and re-solve the equation.

Examples of finding inverses: Find the inverse of $f(x) = 2x + 1$

$f(x) = 2x + 1$
$y = 2x + 1$
$x = 2y + 1$
$y = \dfrac{x - 1}{2}$

This was a simple example which didn't involve many complex operations. Sometimes finding inverses can be more difficult.

Find the inverse of $f(x) = \log_5(x - 7) + 1$

$f(x) = \log_5(x - 7) + 1$
$y = \log_5(x - 7) + 1$
$x = \log_5(y - 7) + 1$
$x - 1 = \log_5(y - 7)$
$5^{x-1} = (y - 7)$
$y = 5^{x-1} + 7$

$f^{-1}(x) = 5^{x-1} + 7$

Representations of Functions: Symbolic, Graphical, and Tabular

What is "slope" and how do you find it? Slope refers to the steepness of the line. The slope-intercept form is $y = mx + b$ where "m" is the slope.

$$m = \left(\dfrac{y_2 - y_1}{x_2 - x_1}\right) = \dfrac{"rise"}{"run"}$$

How do you find the "x" and "y" intercepts? To find the x-intercept, set $y = 0$ and solve for x. To find the y-intercept, set $x = 0$ and solve for y.

Example: Find the slope and *x* & *y* intercepts from the following table of numbers.

X	Y
0	2
1	3
2	4
3	5
4	6

Slope = (3-2)/(1-0) = 1/1 = 1

X-intercept = -2

Y-intercept = 2

How do you graph Linear Equations in TWO variables?

You can think of each "*x*" and "*y*" value as an **ordered pair (*x,y*)** in a graph.

Follow these five steps:
1. Solve the equation for *Y*. (This means to have *Y* by itself on one side and have a coefficient of 1.)
2. Arbitrarily pick a value for *X*.
3. Plug that *X* value into the equation and solve for *Y*.
4. Repeat this process until you have a minimum of three ordered pairs.
5. Draw a straight line to connect the plotted points.

Question: Graph $x + y = 10$

1.) Solve the equation for *y* by moving "*x*" to the other side of the equation. Since the *x* term is positive then we subtract *x* from each side.

$$x + y = 10$$
$$(x - x) + y = (10 - x)$$
$$y = 10 - x$$

2.) Arbitrarily pick a value for *X*.

3.) Plug it into the equation to find *y*.

   Let's try $x = 0$.

$$y = 10 - x$$
$$y = 10 - 0$$
$$y = 10$$

Therefore, our first ordered pair is (0, 10).

4.) Repeat the process until you have a minimum of three ordered pairs.

   Try $x = 1$
$$y = 10 - x$$
$$y = 10 - 1$$
$$y = 9$$

Therefore, our second ordered pair is (1, 9).

   Try $x = 2$
$$y = 10 - x$$
$$y = 10 - 2$$
$$y = 8$$

Therefore, our third ordered pair is (2, 8).

5.) Draw a straight line to connect the plotted points. Here is the graph you should have created.

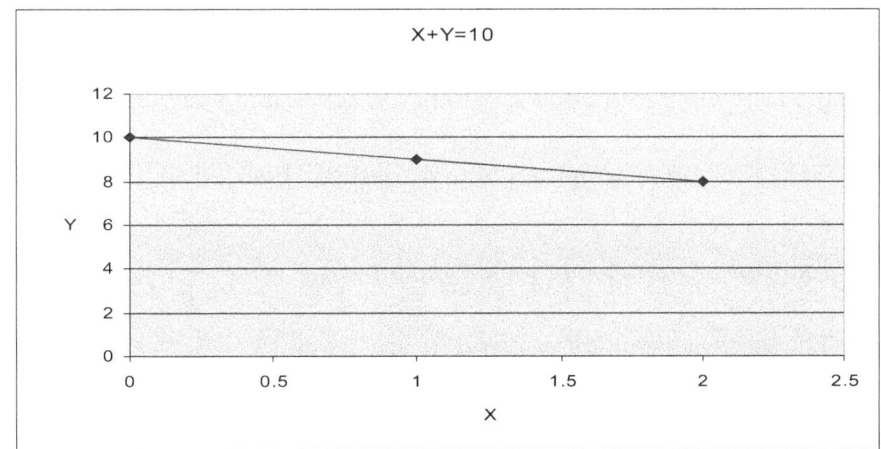

How do you graph a quadratic equation? The graph of a quadratic equation is a parabola. You can graph a quadratic equation by setting $y = ax^2 + bx + c$. Arbitrarily pick a value for x, plug this into the equation to find y. Graph the coordinate pairs.

Note: If "a" is positive then the parabola will open upward. If "a" is negative then the parabola will open downward. The "vertex" of the parabola is the lowest point on the parabola that opens upward or the highest point on the parabola that opens downward. A parabola should be symmetric with a vertical line of symmetry that splits the two halves of the parabola.

Note: You can find the vertex of the parabola using $x = -\dfrac{b}{2a}$ and $y = \dfrac{4ac - b^2}{4a}$

Question: Graph $y = x^2$
If $x = 3$ then $y = 9$. If $x = 4$ then $y = 16$. If $x = 5$ then $y = 25$.
If $x = -3$ then $y = 9$. If $x = -4$ then $y = 16$. If $x = -5$ then $y = 25$.

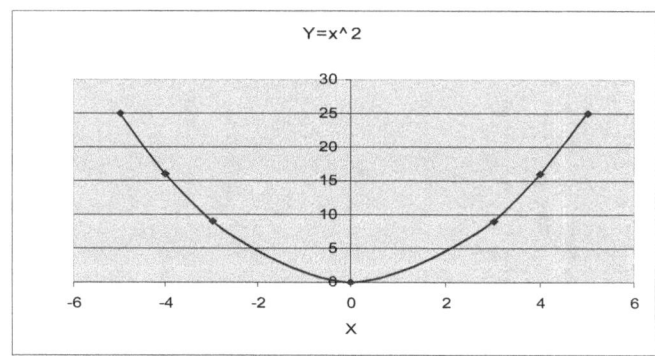

How do you graph systems of linear equations? Simply graph a line for each linear equation.

How do you graph Rational Functions? To graph a rational function you need to find the following: asymptotes, symmetry, zeros, and y intercept if they exist.

NOTE: Graph asymptotes with a "dashed" line.

Example: Graph the rational function: $R(x) = \dfrac{3}{x^2 - 1}$

The vertical asymptotes would be at $x = 1$ and $x = -1$.
The horizontal asymptote would be $y = 0$.

There are no holes. (**Holes** are the values for *x* for which both $P(x)$ and $Q(x) = 0$.)

Determine a few values of $R(x)$ by plugging in values for *x*. For example, if $x = 2$ then $R(x) = 1$. When $x = 0$ then $R(x) = -3$.

The graph of this Rational function will look like the following:

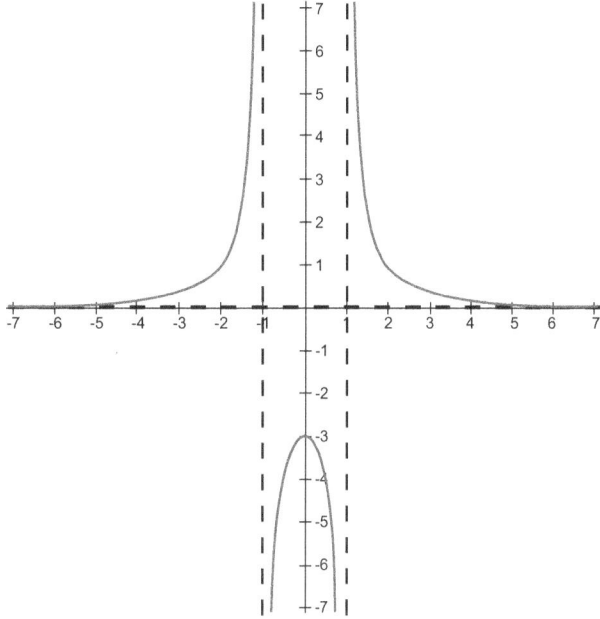

Graphing linear functions: Linear functions are the simplest to graph because they take the form of a line. The most common form you will find linear functions in is the form $y = mx + b$. In this form "m" represents the slope of the equation and "b" represents the *y*-intercept (where it crosses the *y* axis). If *b* is positive it will represent an upward translation. If *b* is negative it will represent a downward translation.

Graphing quadratic functions: A quadratic function is better recognized as a parabola. If the x^2 is positive, the graph will appear as a parabola (curve) which opens upward. If it is negative, it will appear as a parabola which opens downward. The most basic parabola is $y = x^2$. This parabola has a vertex at (0,0). The vertex is the lowest point on the graph. It can be located visually or by looking at the equation. For a quadratic function $y = c(x - a)^2 + b$ the vertex will be (a, b). This is because numbers which are "inside" the square with the x will result in a horizontal translation. If "a" is positive the translation will be to the left, and if "a" is negative the translation will be to the right. Numbers which are "outside" the square (such as b in the prior example) will result in vertical translations. A positive value for b will result in an upward translation, and a negative value will result in a downward translation. The "c" in the equation will stretch the graph so that it is taller and thinner (if $c > 1$) or so that it is flatter and wider (if $c < 1$).

Example: Determine the vertex of and graph the function $y = (x + 2)^2 - 1$.

Answer: The vertex can be determined from the equation as $(-2, -1)$. Because the "x^2" is positive it opens upward. Therefore, the approximate graph is

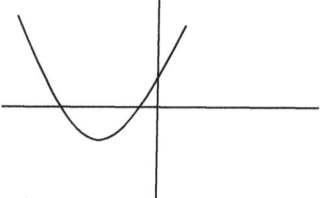

Graphing absolute value functions: The graph of an absolute value appears as a "V." A general form for absolute value equations is $y = a|x - b| + c$. As with quadratic equations, you can determine the vertex (when the "V" comes together) by looking at the equation. It is the point (b, c). The value of b affects the equation because it shifts the absolute value in the horizontal direction. If $b > 0$ (the value is subtracted from x) the result will be a rightward translation. If $b < 0$ the translation will be to the left. Vertical translations are created by c, or the value outside of the absolute value. If $c > 0$, the translation will be upward, and if $c < ,0$ the translation will be downward. The value "a" can have two different effects on the graph. Firstly, a can stretch the graph to be taller and thinner if it is greater than one, or it can make the graph wider and flatter if it is a fraction (i.e., $0 < a < 1$). Secondly, if "a" is negative instead of positive it will flip the absolute value upside down so that it opens downward instead of upward.

Example: Determine the vertex of and graph the function $y = -2|x + 1| + 2$

Answer: The vertex is determined from the equation as $(-1, 2)$. Because the absolute value is multiplied by two, the graph will be taller and thinner than it would be otherwise. It will also open downward because the two is negative. Therefore, the approximate graph of the equation is:

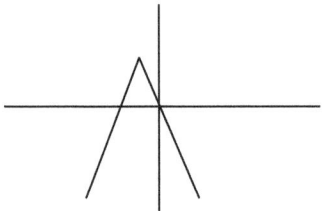

Graphing exponential equations: Exponential equations can be simple to graph if you keep in mind a couple of little tips. A general form for exponential equations is $y = ax - b + c$. The most basic exponential graph is that of $y = 2x$. This graph will have a y intercept of 1, will increase exponentially to the right of the y axis, and will approach a horizontal asymptote of the x axis to the left of the y axis. In other words, the basic shape of any exponential graph is:

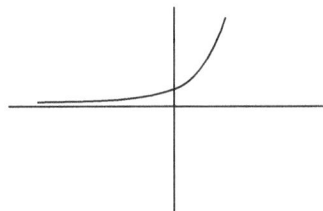

This graph can be altered in the following ways:

- a: the base of the exponential figure will determine how steeply it increases and how sharp the curve in it is. Higher bases will be more sharply curved and steeply sloped.
- b: the number that is actually in the exponent will be responsible for horizontal shifts. If the b value is being subtracted from the x than it will result in a rightward shift. If it is added than it will be leftward.
- c: the c value which is added/subtracted at the end of the equation will be responsible for upward and downward shifts. Positive values represent upward shifts, negative values represent downward shifts.
- x: if the x in the exponent is negative this indicates that the graph should be reflected across the y axis (it would increase exponentially to the left and approach zero to the right).

How to graph logarithmic equations: The graphs of logarithmic equations and exponential functions are closely related as the two operations are inverses of each other. As you may remember from the section on inverse, a function and its inverse are mirrors of each other over the line $y = x$ when graphed. The following figure demonstrates this with the basic exponential function shown as a dotted line, and the corresponding basic logarithmic graph shown in a solid line.

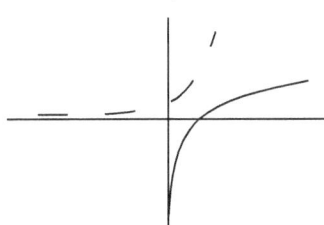

The basic formula for a logarithmic graph is $\log_a(x - b) + c$. This graph can be altered in the following ways:

- a: the base of the logarithm will determine how steeply it increases and how sharp the curve in it is. Higher bases will be more sharply curved and steeply sloped.

b: the number that is actually in the logarithm will be responsible for horizontal shifts. If the *b* value is being subtracted from the *x* than it will result in a rightward shift. If it is added than it will be leftward.

c: the *c* value which is added/subtracted at the end of the equation will be responsible for upward and downward shifts. Positive values represent upward shifts, negative values represent downward shifts.

x: if the *x* in the logarithm is negative this indicates that the graph should be reflected across the y axis (it would increase exponentially to the left and approach the y axis to the right).

What do graphs of trigonometric functions look like? There are a variety of trigonometric functions including: sine, cosine, tangent, arcsine, arccosine, arctangent, cosecant, secant, and cotangent. Trigonometric functions tend to have a repeating pattern.

Following is an example of the sine and cosine functions. **Sine is BLUE** and **Cosine is RED**.

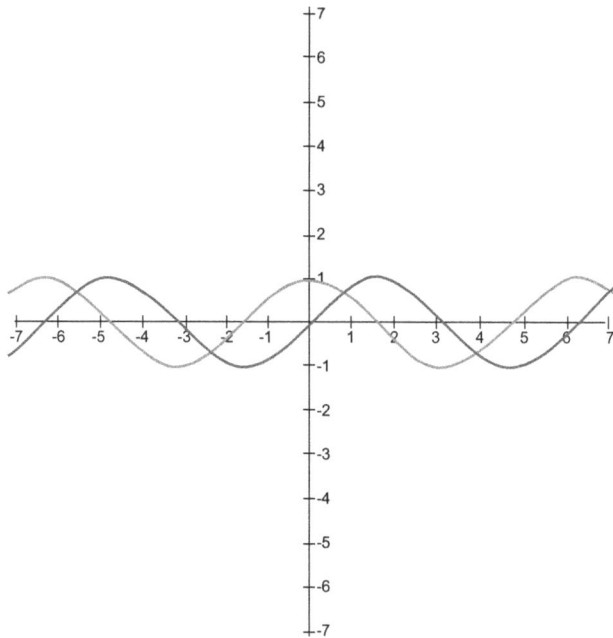

Graphing sine: As you can see in the image above, the graph of sine is essentially a continuous wave which starts at (0, 0) and radiates outward in both directions. To understand this graph some basic wave terminology must be understood.

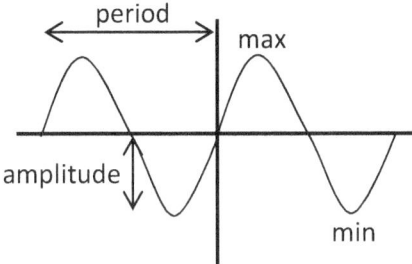

Period: The length of a single cycle of the sine curve (once cycle involved going up and going down before it repeats again).

Min/max: the low and high points of the wave.

Amplitude: The height of the wave (from the axis to the min or the axis to the max).

The general formula for a sine function is $y = A sin(Bx + C) + D$. The basic sine curve (represented by the equation $y - sin(x)$) has the characteristics of a period of 2π, and an amplitude of one. The graph is manipulated in the following ways:

A: The number before the "sine" represents the amplitude. A higher value of A will make the graph taller and thinner. A fractional value will make it flatter and shorter. A negative value will reflect it across the x axis.

B: B is used in determining the period. Period is found with the formula $2\pi/B$. Therefore, when B is large the graph will have a small period and will oscillate more frequently. When B is fractional the graph will have a large period and will have wider oscillations.

C: C represents horizontal shifts in the graph. If the C value is added, the graph shifts left. If it is subtracted, the graph shifts right.

D: The D value represents vertical shifts. If the D value is added, the result is an upward shift. If it is subtracted the result is a downward shift.

Graphing cosine: Cosine follows all of the same rules as sine does, however instead of originating at the origin, it originates at the point (0, 1) and radiates downward first in both directions.

Following is the graph of the **tangent** function.

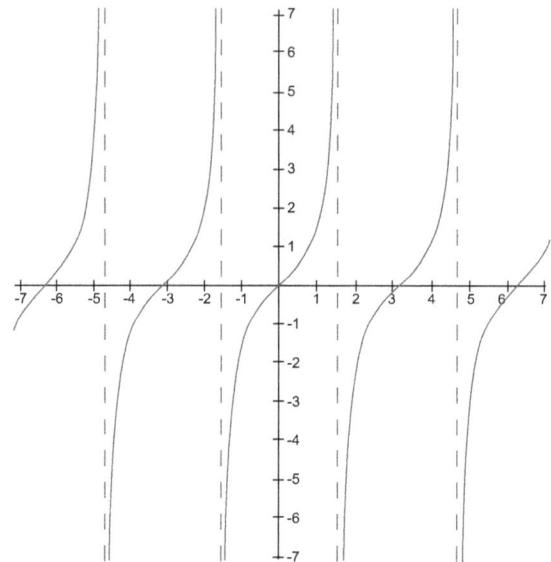

Graphing tangent: The graph of tangent is a repetitive graph as are sine and cosine, however it has a series of vertical asymptotes which it approaches. The graph originates at the origin and radiates outward in both directions, as the sine function does. However, instead of curving back towards the axis, the function increases to positive and negative infinity as it approaches asymptotes. These asymptotes will fall at all of the values of pi (0,π,2π,3π,etc).

Following is an example of the arcsine and arccosine functions. **Arcsine is BLUE** and **Arccosine is RED**.

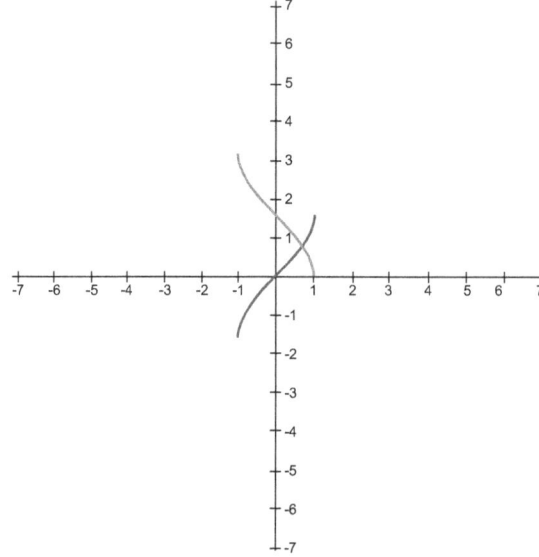

Graphing arcsine and arccosine: Arcsine and arccosine are the inverses of sine and cosine. Therefore they are reflections of the two graphs. Essentially arcsine and arccosine are sine and cosine graphs that run vertically rather than horizontally. However, in order to remain functions, only half of a cycle can be shown (otherwise it would fail the vertical line test). Therefore, their domains are restricted for graphing purposes. This is also true of arctangent.

Following is the graph of the **arctangent** function:

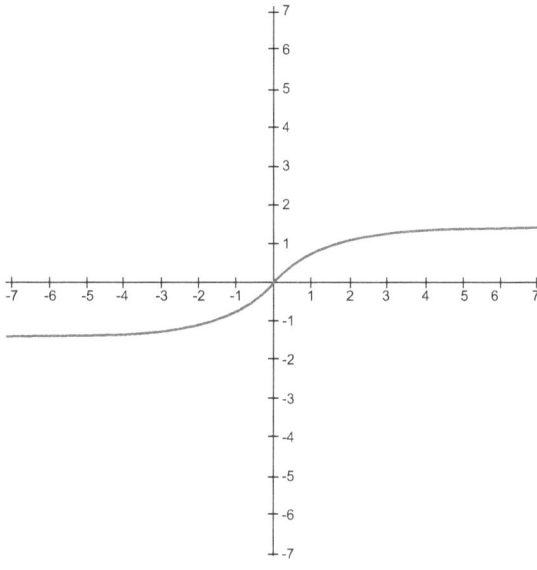

What are "piecewise-defined" functions? Piecewise-defined functions are functions that are split up. Different pieces of the function will yield different graphs.

Example: Graph $f(x) = \begin{cases} x^2 - 2 \text{ for x } \leq -1 \\ x + 3 \text{ for x} > -1 \end{cases}$

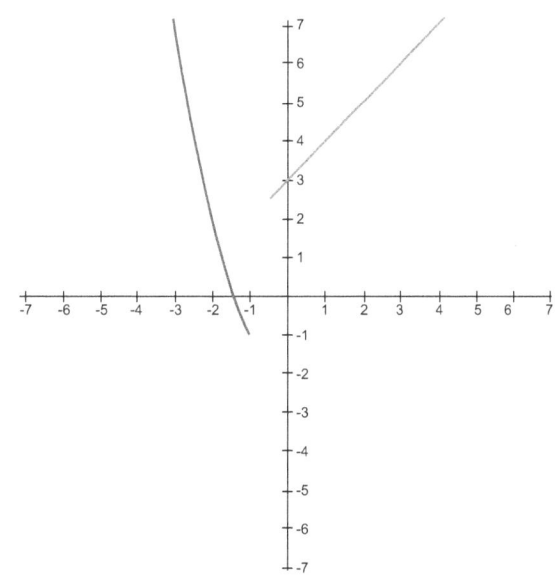

What are "transformations" on functions? Transformations on functions refer to moving the graph of the function around on the axis. The formal definition is that a transformation is when you assign each point in the plane a different point or the point itself.

A graph can be moved through reflections, translations, and rotations.

Reflections: Reflections are transformations across a line of symmetry.

The following graph is a Reflection about the *y*-axis:

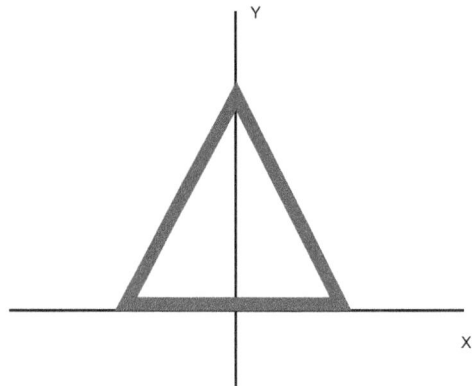

Translations: A translation is a transformation of the plane such that the image of every point (*a*,*b*) is the point (*a* + *h*, *b* + *k*) where *h* and *k* are given.

Example: A translation of a triangle.

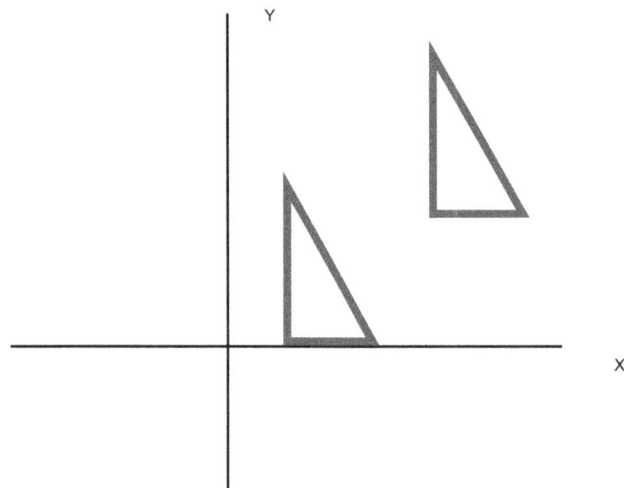

Rotations: A rotation through an angle of measure δ degrees about a point *P*.

Example: A rotation of a triangle.

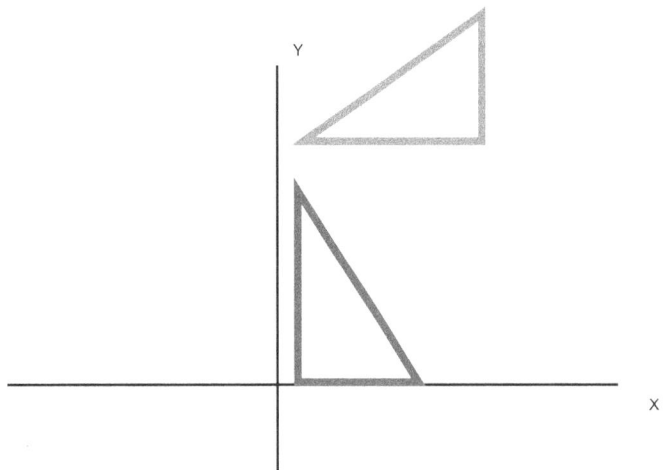

Analytical Geometry

What terms are associated with a "Circle"? Common terms associated with a circle include: radius, diameter, circumference, chord, central angle, arc, and major and minor arcs.

Radius – The radius of a circle is a line segment joining the center to a point on the circle.

Diameter – The diameter of a circle is twice the radius. It is a chord that goes through the center of the circle.

Circumference – The circumference of a circle is the distance around a circle. Note: A circle contains 360°. $C = 2\pi r$ or $C = \pi d$

Chord – A chord of a circle is a line segment that joins two points of the circumference.

Central Angle – The central angle of a circle is an angled formed by two radii.

Arc – The arc of a circle is a continuous part of the circle. The arc *AB* is denoted by $\overline{AB}$. In a circle of radius, *r*, the length *l* of an arc of measure *n*° is $l = \dfrac{n}{360} 2 \; r = \dfrac{nr}{180}$

Major arc – A major arc is an arc that is greater than a semicircle. **Minor Arc** – A minor arc is an arc that is less than a semicircle.

Following is a visual representation of the terms associated with a circle:

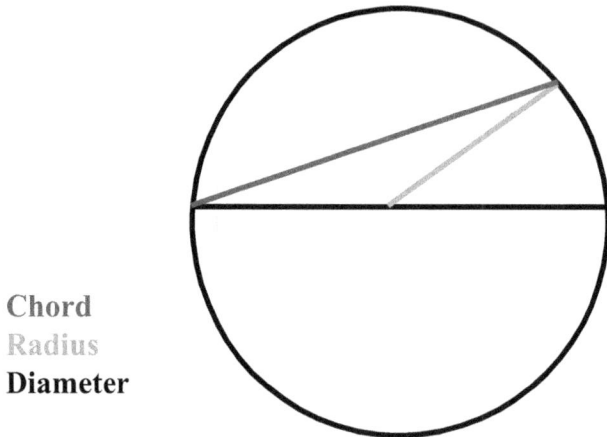

Chord
Radius
Diameter

What is the standard form of the equation of a circle? $(x-h)^2 + (y-k)^2 = r^2$

 Parabola

What is a parabola? A parabola is the locus of all points in a plane equidistant from a fixed line, the directrix, and a fixed point, the focus. In other words, the graph of a quadratic equation is a parabola. You can graph a quadratic equation by setting $y = ax^2 + bx + c$. Arbitrarily pick a value for *x*, plug this into the equation to find *y*. Graph the coordinate pairs.

Note: If "*a*" is positive then the parabola will open upward. If "a" is negative then the parabola will open downward. The "vertex" of the parabola is the lowest point on the parabola that opens upward or the highest point on the parabola that opens downward. A parabola should be symmetric with a vertical line of symmetry that splits the two halves of the parabola.

Note: You can find the vertex of the parabola using $x = -\dfrac{b}{2a}$ and $y = \dfrac{4ac - b^2}{4a}$

Question: Graph $y = x^2$

If $x = 3$ then $y = 9$. If $x = 4$ then $y = 16$. If $x = 5$ then $y = 25$.

If $x = -3$ then $y = 9$. If $x = -4$ then $y = 16$. If $x = -5$ then $y = 25$.

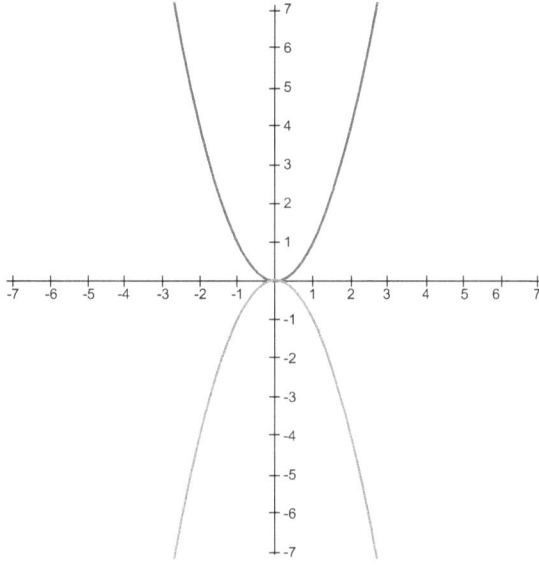

$Y = x^2$

$Y = -x^2$

Ellipse

What is an ellipse? An ellipse is the locus of all points in a plane such that the sum of the distances from two fixed points, the foci, to any point on the locus is constant.

Following are the standard forms for the central ellipses:

$$\frac{x^2}{a^2} + \frac{y^2}{b^2} = 1 \quad \text{and} \quad \frac{y^2}{a^2} + \frac{x^2}{b^2} = 1.$$ Ellipses look like

How to graph ellipses: Essentially the graph of an ellipse will always look like a flattened or a squished circle as the case may be. A general formula for ellipses is

$$\frac{(x-h)^2}{a^2} + \frac{(y-k)^2}{b^2} = 1$$

Once the equation is in this formula, the following can be determined:
If $a > b$ than the major axis (or longer axis) will be the x direction, and the oval will be wider horizontally than it is vertically. If $b > a$, than the opposite is true.
    a: the value of a determined through the equation is the length of the axis in the x direction. The axis will be the distance from the center, or vertex, to the outer edge of the ellipse.
    b: the value of b determined from the equation will be the distance from the center, or vertex, to the outer edge of the ellipse in both directions in the vertical direction (i.e., the entire length of the axis will be $2b$).
    (h, k): this will be the location of the center or vertex of the ellipse.

Hyperbola

What is a hyperbola? A hyperbola is the locus of all points in a plane such that for any point of the locus the difference of the distances from two fixed points, the foci, is constant. Central hyperbolas have their center at the origin. **Note:** Hyperbolas look like two parabolas that are reflected over a line of symmetry.

Following are the standard forms for central hyperbolas:

$$\frac{x^2}{a^2} - \frac{y^2}{b^2} = 1 \quad \text{and} \quad \frac{y^2}{a^2} - \frac{x^2}{b^2} = 1.$$

How to graph hyperbolas: Graphing hyperbolas is actually somewhat similar to graphing ellipses because the two share such similar equations. Hyperbolas can open vertically (one parabola going upward and one going downward) or they can open horizontally (one opening to the left and one to the right. The equations for the two are slightly different. The general form for a hyperbola graph is:

Horizontal Hyperbola:	Vertical Hyperbola:
$\frac{(x-h)^2}{a^2} - \frac{(y-k)^2}{b^2} = 1$	$\frac{(y-k)^2}{a^2} - \frac{(x-h)^2}{b^2} = 1$

Note: a is always greater than b. Therefore, horizontal hyperbolas will be divided by a larger number under the x, and it will come first. Vertical hyperbolas will be divided by a larger number under the y and the y will come first.

Also note: The difference between the formula for a hyperbola and the formula for an ellipse is that the hyperbola equation has a subtracted sign and the ellipse formula has an addition sign.

Once the equation is in this standard form, the following can be determined:
(*h*, *k*): This point will be the center. Be aware that the center of a hyperbola and the vertex are two totally different things. Because hyperbolas are composed of two opposite outward facing parabolas, the center is at the middle of the two, whereas the vertex is point of the parabolas closest to the center.
(*h*±*a*, *k*): The vertices of a horizontal hyperbola.
(*h*, *k*±*a*): The vertices of a vertical parabola.

Trigonometry and Its Applications

There are several trigonometry "identities" that help you when you are working with right triangles and the unit circle. These identities allow you to determine unknown angles and unknown lengths of line segments.

What are the basic Trigonometric Identities? Following is a list of basic trigonometric identities:

$$sinA = \frac{opposite}{hypotenuse} \qquad cosA = \frac{adjacent}{hypotenuse} \qquad tanA = \frac{opposite}{adjacent}$$

The terms "opposite", "adjacent", and "hypotenuse" come from the Right Triangle. Following is a visual representation of these terms.  is the acute angle A.

Right Triangle:

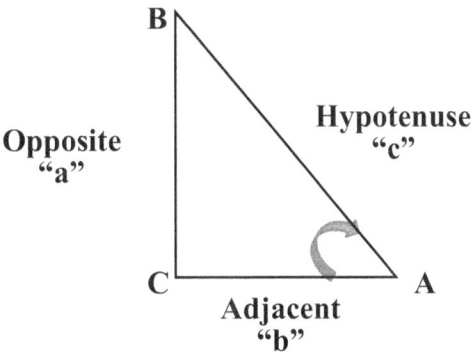

The trigonometric identities also have inverses. The inverse of *sin* is *csc*. The inverse of *cos* is *sec*, and the inverse of *tan* is *cot*.

$$csc\, A = \frac{hypotenuse}{opposite} \qquad sec\, A = \frac{hypotenuse}{adjacent} \qquad cot\, A = \frac{adjacent}{opposite}$$

NOTE: Sometimes you work in "Degrees" while other times you will work in "Radians". A **degree** is a unit of angular measure in which a complete revolution is 360°. A **radian** (rad) is a unit of angular measure in which a complete revolution measure 2π radians.

How do you convert between degrees and radians? Use the following conversion:

$$1 \text{ revolution} = 360° = 2\pi \text{ rad}$$

$$1 \text{ rad} = \frac{180°}{\pi} = \frac{1}{2\pi} \text{ revolution}$$

$$1° = \frac{\pi}{180°} \text{ rad} = \frac{1}{360} \text{ revolution}$$

Special Right Triangles:

A 30 – 60 – 90 right triangle is a special right triangle. You can find the side lengths and angle measures using the following diagram.

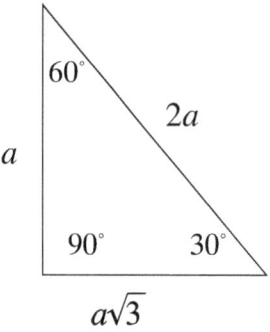

A 45 – 45 – 90 right triangle is a special right triangle. You can find the side lengths and angle measures using the following diagram.

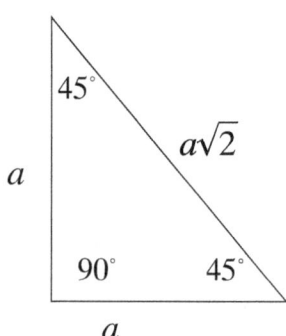

What is the "Unit Circle"? Trigonometric identities can also be derived from the Unit Circle. The Unit Circle is a circle centered at the origin with a radius = 1.

You can draw an angle and it will give you a point on the unit circle. The point is called P and has x and y coordinates. $P=(x,y)$

An angle on the unit circle is defined as π.

A visual representation of the unit circle looks like the following:

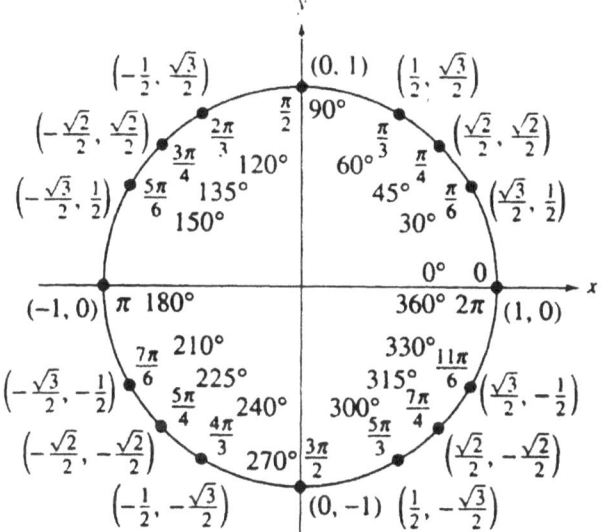

 Trigonometric Functions Based on the Unit Circle

1. **Sine:** $\sin\pi = y$, the y-coordinate of P. For all π $-1 \leq \sin\pi \leq 1$.

2. **Cosine:** $\cos\pi = x$, the x-coordinate of P. For all π $-1 \leq \cos\pi \leq 1$.

3. **Tangent:** $\tan\pi = y/x$, the slope of the line from the origin to point P.

4. **Secant:** $\sec\pi = 1/x = 1/\cos\pi$

5. **Cosecant:** $\csc\pi = 1/y = 1/\sin\pi$

6. **Cotangent:** $\cot\pi = x/y = 1/\tan\pi = \cos\pi/\sin\pi$

Formulas to Memorize

PYTHAGOREAN IDENTITIES

$\sin^2\theta + \cos^2\theta = 1$

$\tan^2\theta + 1 = \sec^2\theta$

$1 + \cot^2\theta = \csc^2\theta$

CO-FUNCTION IDENTITIES

$\cos\left(\frac{\pi}{2} - x\right) = sinx$

$\sin\left(\frac{\pi}{2} - x\right) = cosx$

$\tan\left(\frac{\pi}{2} - x\right) = cotx$

$\csc\left(\frac{\pi}{2} - x\right) = secx$

$\sec\left(\frac{\pi}{2} - x\right) = cscx$

HALF-ANGLE FORMULAS

$\sin\left(\frac{x}{2}\right) = \pm\sqrt{\frac{1 - cosx}{2}}$

$\cos\left(\frac{x}{2}\right) = \pm\sqrt{\frac{1 + cosx}{2}}$

$\tan\left(\frac{x}{2}\right) = \pm\frac{1 - cosx}{sinx}$

DOUBLE ANGLE FORMULAS

$sin2\theta = 2sin\theta cos\theta$

$cos2\theta = cos^2\theta - sin^2\theta = 1 - 2sin^2\theta$
$\qquad\qquad = 2cos^2\theta - 1$

$tan2\theta = \frac{2tan\theta}{1 - tan^2\theta}$

LAW OF SINES

$\frac{a}{sinA} = \frac{b}{sinB} = \frac{c}{sinC}$

LAW OF COSINES

$$a^2 = b^2 + c^2 - 2bc\cos A$$
$$A = \cos^{-1}\left(\frac{b^2 + c^2 - a^2}{2bc}\right)$$

EVEN/ODD IDENTITIES

$\sin(-x) = -\sin x$
$\cos(-x) = \cos(x)$
$\tan(-x) = -\tan(x)$

RECIPROCAL IDENTITIES

$\csc x = \dfrac{1}{\sin x}$
$\sec x = \dfrac{1}{\cos x}$
$\cot x = \dfrac{1}{\tan x}$

SUM AND DIFFERENCE FORMULAS

$\sin(x \pm y) = \sin x \cos y \pm \cos x \sin y$

$\cos(x \pm y) = \cos x \cos y \pm \sin x \sin y$

$\tan(x \pm y) = \dfrac{\tan x \pm \tan y}{1 \pm \tan x \tan y}$

SUM-TO-PRODUCT FORMULAS

$\sin x \pm \sin y = 2 \sin\left(\dfrac{x \pm y}{2}\right) \cos\left(\dfrac{x \pm y}{2}\right)$

$\cos x + \cos y = 2 \cos\left(\dfrac{x + y}{2}\right) \cos\left(\dfrac{x - y}{2}\right)$

$\cos x \cos y = -2 \sin\left(\dfrac{x + y}{2}\right) \sin\left(\dfrac{x - y}{2}\right)$

PRODUCT-TO-SUM FORMULAS

$\sin x \cdot \sin y = \dfrac{1}{2}[\cos(x - y) - \cos(x + y)]$

$\cos x \cdot \cos y = \dfrac{1}{2}[\cos(x - y) + \cos(x + y)]$

$\sin x \cdot \cos y = \dfrac{1}{2}[\sin(x + y) + \sin(x - y)]$

$\cos x \cdot \sin y = \dfrac{1}{2}[\sin(x + y) - \sin(x - y)]$

Sample Test Questions

ALGEBRAIC EXPRESSIONS, EQUATIONS, AND INEQUALITIES
(20 QUESTIONS)

1) Add $(7x + 3y^3 - 4xy) + (3x - 2y^3 + 7xy)$

   A) $4x + 5y^3 + 3xy$
   B) $10x + y^3 + 3xy$
   C) $21x - 6y^3 - 28xy$
   D) $4x - 5y^3 - 3x^2y^2$

2) Evaluate $4x^3y^2 - 3xz^2$ given $x = -1$, $y = 3$, $z = 2$

   A) -24
   B) 48
   C) -48
   D) 12

3) Simplify $1 + x^2 + 6 - 3x^2$

   A) $-3x^4 + 7$
   B) $-2x^2 + 7$
   C) $4x^2 + 6$
   D) $-2x^2 + 6$

4) Simplify $3(x - 5) - x$

   A) $3x - 15$
   B) $3x - 15 - x$
   C) $2x - 15$
   D) $3x^2 - 8 + x$

5) Simplify $\frac{1}{2}(x+3) + \frac{1}{3}(3x+6)$

   A) $\frac{1}{5}x + 18$

   B) $\frac{1}{10}x + \frac{3}{2} + x + 2$

   C) $\frac{3}{2}x + \frac{7}{2}$

   D) $\frac{2}{5}x + \frac{7}{5}$

6) Solve $3x^2 - 4 = 8$

   A) $x = 4, -4$
   B) $x = 2$
   C) $x = 2, -2$
   D) $x = 4$

7) Solve $x^2 - 8x + 7 = 0$

   A) $x = 7, 1$
   B) $x = -7, 1$
   C) $x = 2, 6$
   D) $x = -2, 6$

8) Simplify $(\frac{2y^3}{x})^4$

   A) $\frac{2y^3}{x}$

   B) $\frac{2y^7}{x^4}$

   C) $\frac{16y^{12}}{x^4}$

   D) $\frac{16y^7}{x^5}$

9) Simplify $(\frac{x^2}{y^3})^{-4}$

   A) $\frac{y^3}{x^2}$

   B) $\frac{y^8}{x^{12}}$

   C) $\frac{y^{12}}{x^8}$

   D) $\frac{y^8}{x^{12}}$

10) Subtract $(5x^2 - x - 1) - (-3x^2 - 2x - 5)$

   A) $8x^2 + x + 4$
   B) $2x^2 - 3x - 6$
   C) $8x^2 - 3x - 6$
   D) $x^2 + 12x + 36$

11) Multiply $(2x + 5)(3x - 6)$

   A) $5x - 11$
   B) $6x^2 - 12x - 1$
   C) $6x^2 - 5x - 11$
   D) $6x^2 + 3x - 30$

12) Multiply $-3x(2x - 2)$

   A) $-x - 5$
   B) $-6x^2 + 6x$
   C) $-6x + 6$
   D) $-5x^2 - 5$

13) A person must determine the time of day at which the shadow cast by a 20 foot tall building is at its longest. They know that as the sun moves across the sky, the angle it hits the building at may be approximated by the values given in the chart below. During which time interval is the shadow cast by the building largest? Note: Assume that during the second half of the day the sun does not hit the building.

Time of Day (AM)	Angle
6:00-7:30	0
7:30-9:00	$\frac{\pi}{6}$
9:00-10:30	$\frac{\pi}{4}$
10:30-12:00	$\frac{\pi}{3}$

A) 6:00-7:30
B) 7:30-9:00
C) 9:00-10:30
D) 10:30-12:00
E) None of the above

14) Solve $-18 = -14 + x$

A) $x = -4$
B) $x = 4$
C) $x = 2$
D) $x = 18$

15) Solve $\frac{x}{8} = -3$

A) $x = 8$
B) $x = -24$
C) $x = -3x$
D) $x = -11$

16) Solve $12 = 4(x - 3)$

    A) $x = 3$
    B) $x = 6$
    C) $x = -3$
    D) $x = -6$

17) Solve $\dfrac{4x + 5}{6} = \dfrac{7}{2}$

    A) $x = 4$
    B) $x = 12$
    C) $x = 2$
    D) $x = 3$

18) Solve $-12 \quad -3x$

    A) $x \leq 4$
    B) $x \geq 4$
    C) $x \geq -4$
    D) $x \leq -4$

19) Solve $6(3 - x) < 2x + 12$

    A) $x > \dfrac{3}{4}$
    B) $x < \dfrac{3}{4}$
    C) $x > \dfrac{4}{3}$
    D) $x < \dfrac{4}{3}$

20) Determine which ordered pair satisfies the following system of linear equations:

$y = 2x - 3$

$y = x + 5$

A) (8, 13)
B) (4, 5)
C) (4, 9)
D) (8, 9)

Functions: Concept, Properties, and Operations
(15 Questions)

21) Evaluate: $f(g(x))$ when $f(x) = x^2 - 10x + 3$ and $g(x) = 12$

A) 27
B) -14
C) 12
D) 144

22) Evaluate: $f(x) = (x - 2)^2 + 10; f(2)$

A) 14
B) 8
C) 144
D) 10

23) What function can you derive from the following table of data?

x	-2	-1	0	1	2
$f(x)$	-8	-1	0	1	8

A) $f(x) = 4x$
B) $f(x) = x^3$
C) $f(x) = x/3$
D) $f(x) = 3x^3$

24) Evaluate: $f(g(x))$ when $f(x) = 10x$ and $g(x) = x + 4$

   A) 14
   B) $6x$
   C) $x + 4$
   D) $10x + 40$

25) State the domain for $y = -2x + 3$

   A) $\{-2, 0, 1\}$
   B) All real numbers
   C) $\{1, 4, 7\}$
   D) $\{0, 3, 1, 4\}$

26) Find the domain of $\{(-5, -1), (-6, 7), (13, -2)\}$

   A) $\{-1, 7, -2\}$
   B) $\{-5, -6, 13\}$
   C) $\{-5, 13\}$
   D) $\{-2, 7\}$

For Questions 27-29 determine if *y* is a function of *x*.

27) $y = 3x^3$

   A) Yes
   B) No

28) $y^2 = x$

   A) Yes
   B) No

29) $xy = 1$

   A) Yes
   B) No

30) Find the Range of $\{(6, 8), (5, 4)\}$

   A) $\{8, 4\}$
   B) $\{6, 5\}$
   C) $\{4, 8\}$
   D) $\{11, 12\}$

31) If $F(t) = \dfrac{t^3 + 2t}{t - 1}$ find $F(-2)$

   A) -4
   B) 8
   C) 4
   D) 3

32) If $F(x, y) = x^3 - 3xy + y^2$ find $F(2,3)$

   A) -1
   B) 1
   C) 5
   D) -5

33) Find the vertical asymptotes, horizontal asymptotes and holes for the Rational Function:

   $R(x) = \dfrac{3x}{x + 2}$

   A) Vertical: $x = 2$, Horizontal: $y = 1/3$, No holes
   B) Vertical: $x = -2$, Horizontal: $y = 3$, No holes
   C) Vertical: $x = -2$, No Horizontal Asymptote, No holes
   D) Vertical: $x = 4$, Horizontal: $y = 3$, No holes

34) Find the zeros and y intercept for the Rational Function: $R(x) = \dfrac{x^3 - 2x^2 - 3x}{x}$

   A) Zeros: (-3,0) and (1,0); y intercept: None
   B) Zeros: (3,0) and (-1,0); y intercept: 1
   C) Zeros: (3,0) and (-1,0); y intercept: None
   D) Zeros: (3,0) and (-1,0); y intercept: 3

35) Find the asymptotes for the Rational Function: $R(x) = \dfrac{x}{x^2 - 16}$

   A) Vertical: $x = 4$; Horizontal: $y = 0$
   B) Vertical: $x = 4$, $x = -4$; Horizontal: $y = 0$
   C) Vertical: $x = 2$, $x = -2$; Horizontal: $y = 1$
   D) Vertical: $x = 2$, $x = -2$; Horizontal: $y = 16$

Representation of Functions: Symbolic, Graphical, and Tabular
(30 Questions)

36) The following graph represents which Linear Equation?

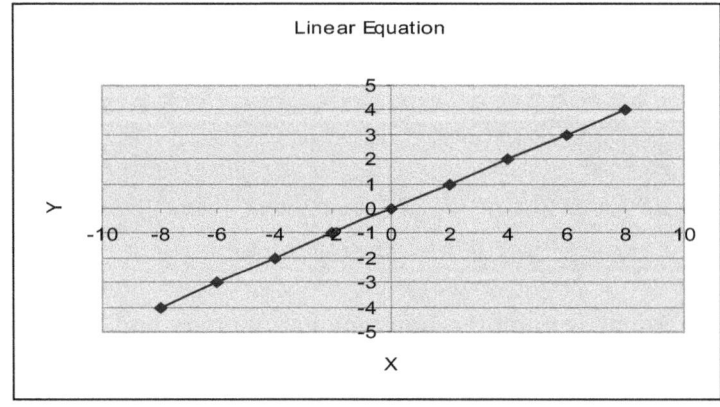

   A) $y = 2x$
   B) $y = x$
   C) $y = x + 2$
   D) $y = \dfrac{1}{2}x$

37) The graph of the quadratic equation $y = x^2 + 4x - 3$ is a parabola that opens…

    A) Upward
    B) Downward

38) Are the graphs of the following systems of equations parallel lines?
$6x - 4y = 12$
$12y = 18x - 24$

    A) Yes
    B) No

39)

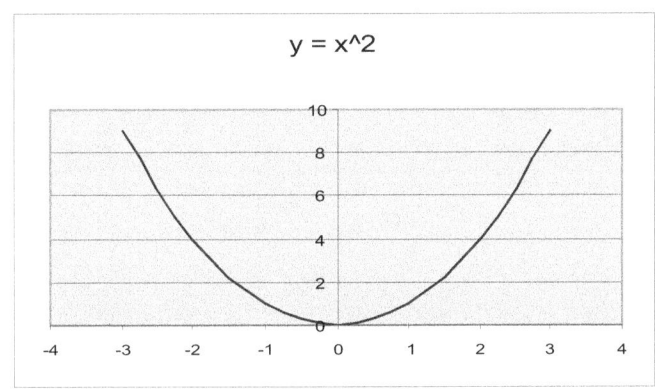

This graph represents the function $f(x) = y = x^2$
This function reflected across the x axis is written as:

    A) $-y = x^2$
    B) $y = -x^2$
    C) $x = y^2$
    D) $-x = y^2$

40) A graph of $x^2 + y^2 = 9$ is a...

   A) Parabola
   B) Hyperbola
   C) Circle
   D) Line

41) Determine whether the function $y = 4x$ is symmetric with respect to the y axis, x axis, or the origin.

   A) y axis
   B) x axis
   C) origin
   D) None

42) Determine whether the function $xy^2 = 1$ is symmetric with respect to the y axis, x axis, or the origin.

   A) y axis
   B) x axis
   C) origin
   D) None

43) Determine whether the function $y = x^3$ is symmetric with respect to the y axis, x axis, or the origin.

   A) y axis
   B) x axis
   C) origin
   D) None

44) Express $4^2 = 16$ in logarithmic form

   A) $2 = \log_4 16$
   B) $4 = \log_4 16$
   C) $2 = \log_2 16$
   D) $4 = \log_2 16$

45) Express $\log_a a^3 = 3$ in exponential form

   A) $3a = a^3$
   B) $a^3 = a$
   C) $\frac{1}{3}a = a^2$
   D) $a^3 = a^3$

46) Solve for x in $3^x = 243$

   A) 7
   B) 6
   C) 15
   D) 5

47) What type of graph would represent the following equation?

$$\frac{(x-4)^2}{9} - \frac{(y-5)^2}{16} = 1$$

   A) Hyperbola
   B) Circle
   C) Line
   D) Parabola

48) What rational function does the following graph represent?

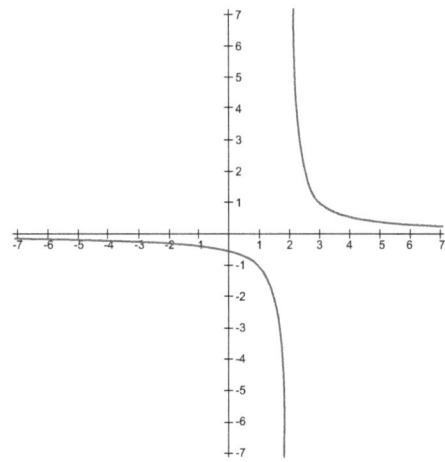

A) $R(x) = \dfrac{x-2}{x^2+4}$

B) $R(x) = \dfrac{x+2}{x^2}$

C) $R(x) = \dfrac{x}{x^2-4}$

D) $R(x) = \dfrac{x+2}{x^2-4}$

49) What rational function does the following graph represent?

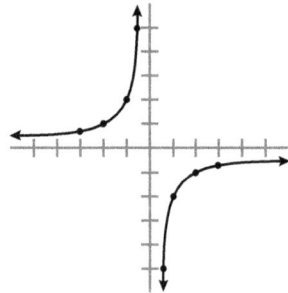

A) $R(x) = \dfrac{x}{2}$

B) $R(x) = \dfrac{2}{x}$

C) $R(x) = 2x$

D) $R(x) = \dfrac{-2}{x}$

50) Determine the slope of the linear equation from the following data:

X	Y
-4	-2
-2	-1
0	0
2	1
4	2

A) 2

B) 1/2

C) -1/2

D) -2

51) The following graph represents what type of transformation?

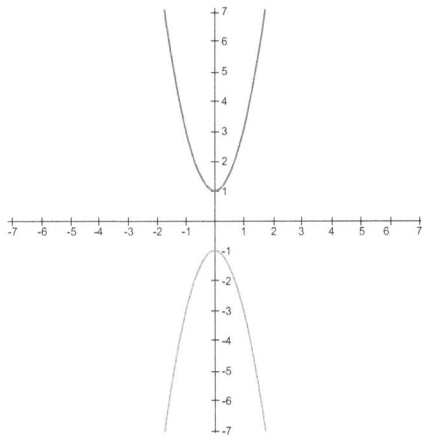

A) Translation

B) Rotation

C) Reflection

D) Dilation

52) What type of function does the following graph represent?

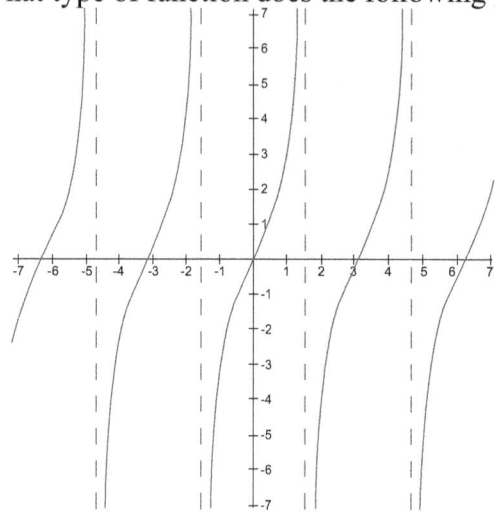

A) Linear
B) Trigonometric
C) Parabola
D) Piecewise

53) What Trigonometric Function is represented in the following graph?

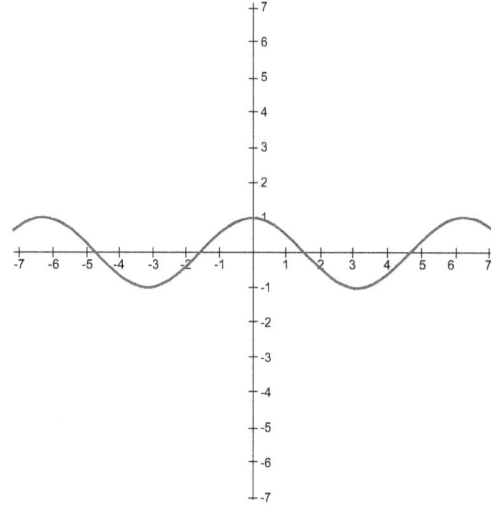

A) Cos(x)
B) Sin(x)
C) Tan(x)

54) What Trigonometric Function is represented in the following graph?

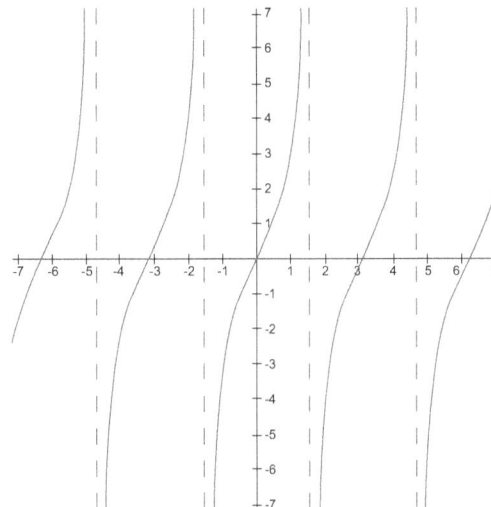

A) Cos(2x)
B) 2sin(x)
C) Csc(2x)
D) 2tan(x)

55) What Trigonometric Function is represented in the following graph?

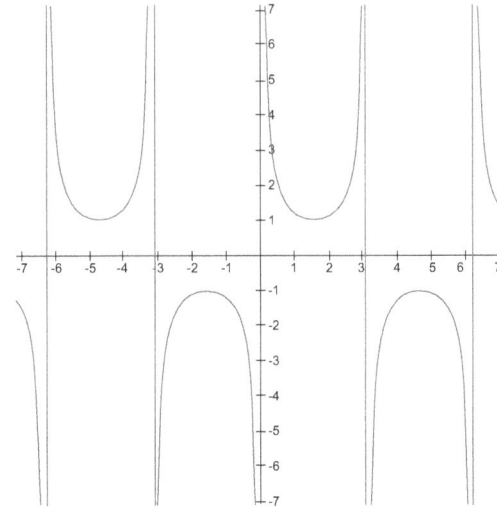

A) Csc(x)
B) Cot(x)
C) Sec(x)
D) Sin(x)

56) A triangle has coordinates (-1,0), (2,0), and (-1,3). What type of transformation occurs if the new coordinates of the triangle are (4,2), (7, 2), (4, 5)?

A) Rotation
B) Reflection
C) Translation
D) Dilation

57) The graph of $y = |x|$ would look like:

A) A "X" that has all positive coordinates
B) A "V" that has all negative coordinates
C) A "X" that has all negative coordinates
D) A "V" that has all positive coordinates

58) Find the solution for the following system of equations based on the graph:

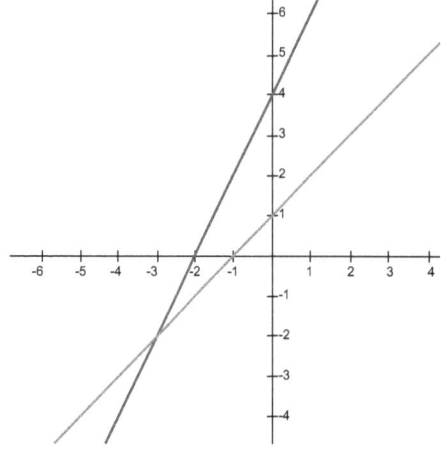

A) (-2,0)
B) (-3, -2)
C) (0,4)
D) (-1,0)

59) Following is the graph of the inequality $y < 2x$.

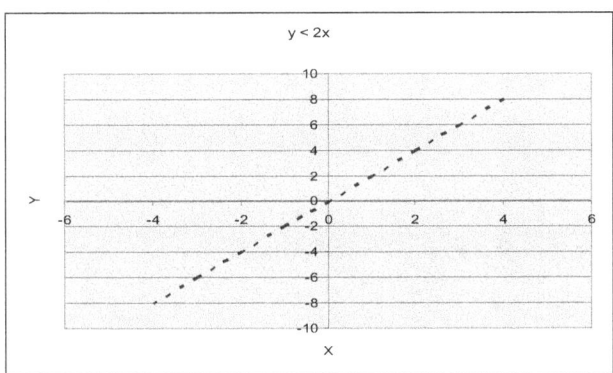

Should you shade the region ABOVE or BELOW the dotted line?

A) ABOVE
B) BELOW

60) What is the line of symmetry for the equation $y = x^2$?

A) $x = 1$
B) $x = -1$
C) $x = \frac{1}{2}$
D) $x = 0$

61) Which equation has a steeper slope: $y = 2x$ or $y = 4x$ or $y = \frac{1}{2}x$?

A) $y = 2x$
B) $y = 4x$
C) $y = \frac{1}{2}x$

62) Determine if the graph of $y = 4x$ is symmetric with respect to the y axis, x axis, or the origin.

A) y axis
B) x axis
C) origin

63) Determine if the graph of $x = y^2 + 1$ is symmetric with respect to the y axis, x axis, or the origin.

   A) y axis
   B) x axis
   C) origin

64) What would the graph of $4x^2 + y^2 = 16$ look like?

   A) Line
   B) Circle
   C) Hyperbola
   D) Ellipse

65) Is -1 a root of the equation $P(x) = x^3 - 7x - 6 = 0$?

   A) Yes
   B) No

Analytical Geometry
(10 Questions)

66) Find the radius of a circle if a 40° arc has a length of 4π.

   A) 18
   B) 36
   C) 40
   D) 12

67) Which equation represents a parabola that has a vertex of (3,0) and a directrix of x=1?

   A) $2(x - 8) = y^2$
   B) $3(x - 0) = y^2$
   C) $8(x - 3) = y^2$
   D) $8(x - 1/3) = y^2$

68) Which equation represents an ellipse that has a center at (2,4), focus at (7,4), and contains the point (5,8)?

A) $\dfrac{(x-7)^2}{49} + \dfrac{(y-4)^2}{16} = 1$

B) $\dfrac{(x)^2}{45} + \dfrac{(y)^2}{20} = 1$

C) $\dfrac{(x-2)^2}{45} + \dfrac{(y-4)^2}{20} = 1$

D) $\dfrac{(x-2)^2}{5} + \dfrac{(y-4)^2}{8} = 1$

69) Which equation represents a hyperbola that has a center at the origin, one vertex at (3,0), and one asymptote at $y = \dfrac{2}{3}x$?

A) $\dfrac{x^2}{9} - \dfrac{y^2}{4} = 1$

B) $\dfrac{x^2}{3} - \dfrac{y^2}{1} = 1$

C) $\dfrac{x^2 - 1}{2} - \dfrac{y^2}{3} = 1$

D) $\dfrac{x^2}{4} - \dfrac{y^2}{6} = 1$

70) How many roots does the following graph contain?

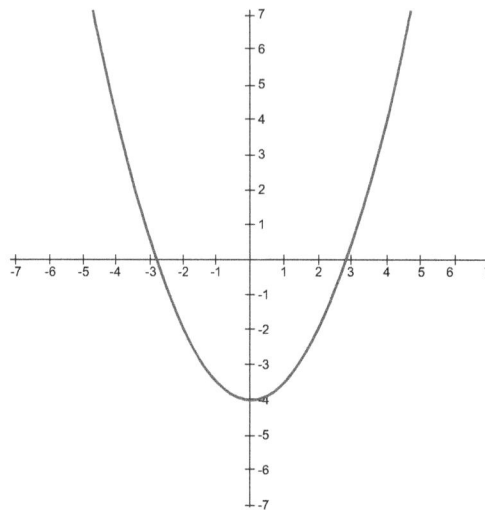

A) 3
B) 0
C) 1
D) 2

71) Find the discriminant $b^2 - 4ac$ of $2x^2 = 5 + 3x$.

A) 49
B) 34
C) 5
D) 42

72) Find the center and radius of a circle from the equation: $(x+2)^2 + (y-4)^2 = 81$

A) C(-2,4), $r = 81$
B) C(-2,4), $r = 9$
C) C(2,-4), $r = 9$
D) C(2,-4), $r = 81$

73) The graph of the equation $xy = 8$ would look like a:

   A) Hyperbola
   B) Line
   C) Parabola
   D) Circle

74) Write the equation of a line through (7,3) that is parallel to the x axis.

   A) $x = 7$
   B) $7x + 3y = 1$
   C) $y = 3$
   D) $3x + 7y = 1$

75) Write the equation of the line that has an x intercept of 6 and a y intercept of 1/3.

   A) $x + 1/3y = 6$
   B) $x + 18y = 3$
   C) $x + 18y = 6$
   D) $x - 18y = 3$

Trigonometry and Its Applications
(15 Questions)

76) Convert 120° into Radians

   A) $\frac{2\pi}{3}$ radians
   B) $\frac{4\pi}{3}$ radians
   C) $\frac{2\pi}{1}$ radians
   D) $\frac{3\pi}{5}$ radians

77) Convert $\frac{2\pi}{5} radians$ into degrees.

    A) 18°
    B) 108°
    C) 72°
    D) 144°

78) Find sinπ if π is an acute angle such that cosπ = 4/5.
    (Hint: Use cosπ² + sinπ² = 1)

    A) 4/5
    B) 3/5
    C) 5/4
    D) 5/3

79) Calculate sin 2π/3

    A) $\frac{\sqrt{3}}{2}$
    B) 12^2
    C) $\frac{\sqrt{9}}{3}$
    D) 2

80) Calculate cos 9π

    A) -1
    B) 1
    C) 9
    D) -9

81) Find the Hypotenuse of a Right triangle given sin = 3/5

   A) 3
   B) 9
   C) 25
   D) 5

82) Find the Hypotenuse of a Right triangle given cos = 4/5

   A) 4
   B) 16
   C) 5
   D) 3

83) In a 30°-60°-90° right triangle what is the length of the Hypotenuse if the sides lengths are 2 and $2\sqrt{3}$?

   A) 2
   B) $\sqrt{3}$
   C) 3
   D) 4

84) The Unit Circle has a radius with a length of?

   A) 1
   B) 2
   C) 4
   D) 0

85) What is the length of the "X" in the following 30°-60°-90° right triangle?

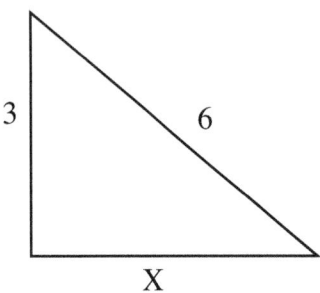

A) $3\sqrt{3}$
B) $6\sqrt{3}$
C) 3
D) 6

86) What is the length of the "X" in the following 45°-45°-90° right triangle?

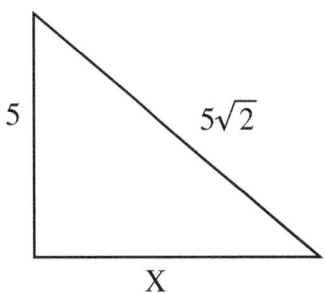

A) $5\sqrt{2}$
B) $\sqrt{2}$
C) 5
D) 10

87) The following graph depicts what trigonometric function and its inverse trigonometric function?

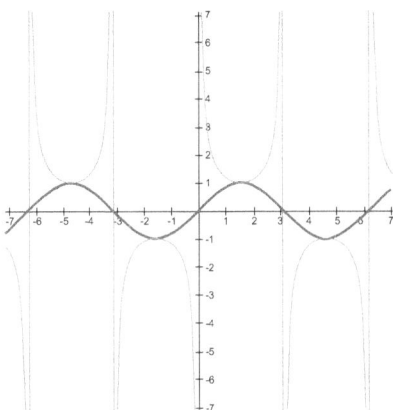

A) cos(x), sin(x)
B) sin(x), csc(x)
C) sin(x), sec(x)
D) sin(x), tan(x)

88) The following graph depicts what trigonometric function and its inverse trigonometric function?

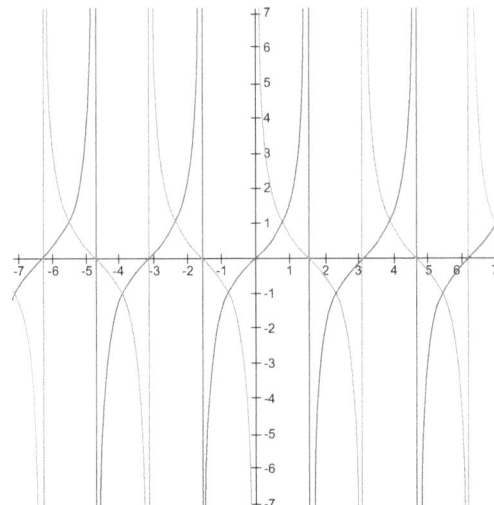

A) tan(x), sin(x)
B) cos(x), sec(x)
C) tan(x), csc(x)
D) tan(x), cot(x)

89) If the cotπ = 4/3 in the Unit circle, how can you express tanπ?

   A) 1
   B) 4/3
   C) 3/4
   D) 9

90) If the cotπ = 4/3 in the Unit circle, how can you express sinπ?

   A) 1
   B) 5/3
   C) 3/5
   D) -3/5

Functions as Models
(10 Questions)

91) If the rate of decay of carbon-14 is 0.0124% per year, how long, rounded to 3 significant digits, will it take for the carbon-14 to diminish to 1% of the original amount after the death of the plant or animal? (Use $A = A_o e^{-rt}$)

   A) 124,000 years
   B) 37,100 years
   C) 17540 years
   D) 24,800 years

92) A right triangle has one leg that is 20 inches in length. The hypotenuse is 10 inches longer than the other leg. Find the length of the hypotenuse.

   A) 25 in.
   B) 15 in.
   C) 20 in.
   D) 35 in.

93) At a local ski resort, Mountain A has a slope = -2 and Mountain B has a slope equal to -1/2. Which Mountain is steeper?

   A) Mountain A
   B) Mountain B

94) A tennis ball is hit in the vertically upward direction with an initial speed of v_0 ft/sec. The projection is given by the formula $s = v_0 t - 16t^2$ where s is the distance at time t sec. If the tennis ball is hit with an initial upward speed of 128 ft/sec, at what times would the tennis ball be 100 ft above the point of project?

   A) 6.95 sec
   B) 1.88 sec, 14.4 sec
   C) 7.12 sec, 0.88 sec
   D) 4 sec

95) Solve the equation given that one root of $x^3 + 2x^2 - 23x - 60 = 0$ is 5.

   A) -5, 3, 4
   B) 5, -3, -4
   C) 1/5, 3, 1/4
   D) 60, 23, 2

96) Write the equation that has the following roots: 5, 1, -3.

   A) $x^3 - 3x^2 - 13x + 15 = 0$
   B) $x^3 + 3x^2 + 13x - 15 = 0$
   C) $3x^3 - x^2 - 15x + 13 = 0$
   D) $3x^3 + 3x^2 + x - 15 = 0$

97) The population of a country grows at a rate of 4% compounded annually. At this rate, how long will it take the population to double? (Use: $A = P(1+\frac{r}{n})^{nt}$)

   A) 8.6 years
   B) 2 years
   C) 17.7 years
   D) 16 years

98) If $1000 is invested at 10% compounded continuously, how long will it take the investment to triple? (Use: $A = Pe^{rt}$ and round to the nearest year.)

   A) 15 years
   B) 11 years
   C) 22 years
   D) 100 years

Use the following graph for questions 99-100:

99) The graph depicts the position of a car in traffic. What type of function does this situation represent?

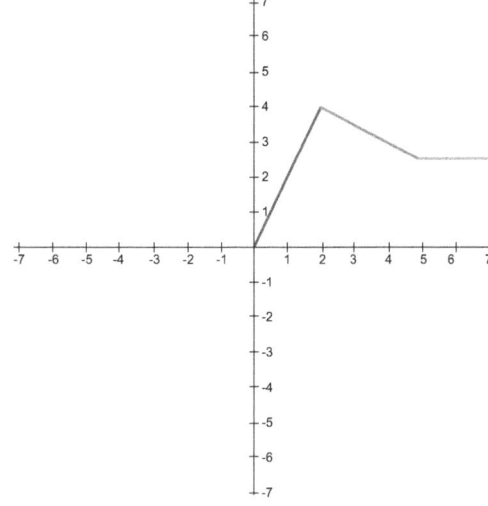

   A) Parabola
   B) Hyperbola
   C) Not a function
   D) Piecewise defined

100) At what interval is the car at a standstill in traffic? (Velocity = 0)?

   A) $5 \leq x \leq 7$
   B) $0 \leq x \leq 2$
   C) $2 \leq x \leq 5$
   D) $0 \leq x \leq 5$

Algebraic Expressions, Equations and Inequalities
(10 Questions)

101) Which of the following graphs correctly demonstrates the solution to the following system of inequalities?

$y > x^2 + 2$
$y \leq 2x + 2$

A)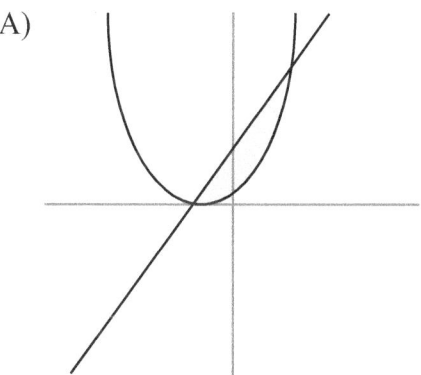

C)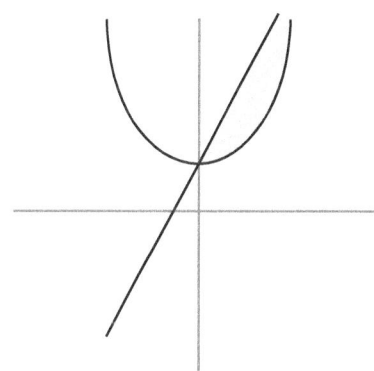

B)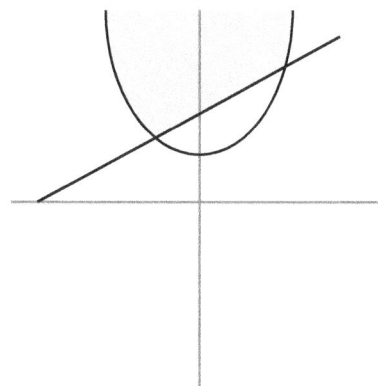

D)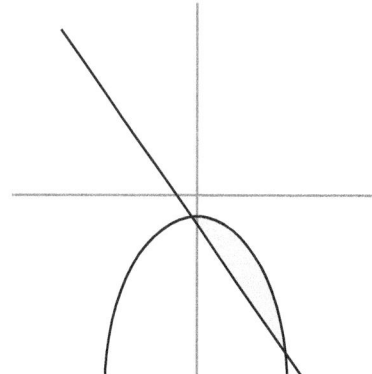

   E) None of the above

102) Find the solution(s) for the following system of equations:

$y = x^2 + 4x + 4$

$y = (x+7)^2$

A) (5,144)

B) (5, 144) and (-5, 144)

C) (0, 49) and (3, 100)

D) (4, 122)

E) None of the above

103) Which of the following graphs correctly demonstrates the solution to the following system of inequalities?

$y \geq |x+5|$

$y < -\dfrac{1}{4}x + 3$

A)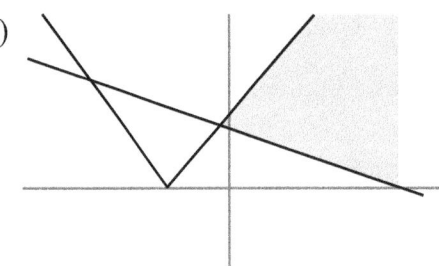

C)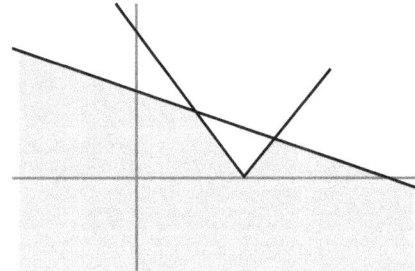

B)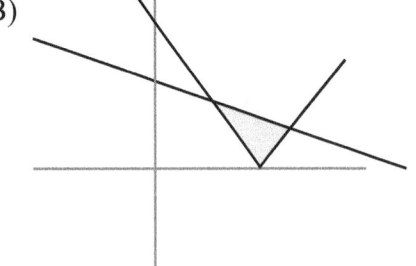

D)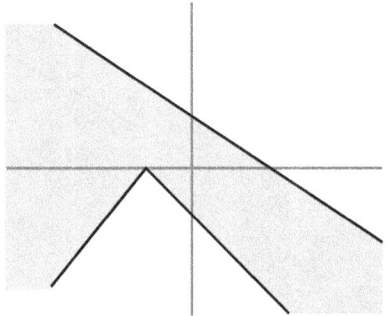

E) None of the above

104) Solve $|x^2 - 3| = 1$

   A) $2, \sqrt{2}\, 8$
   B) ± 2
   C) $\pm 2, \pm \sqrt{2}$
   D) $\pm \sqrt{2}$
   E) $2, -1, 4, \sqrt{2}$

105) Solve $2x^4 - 4x^2 = -2$

   A) $\pm \sqrt{2}$
   B) -1
   C) 1
   D) ± 1
   E) No solution

106) Solve $\ln x + \ln \dfrac{1}{2} = \log 3$

   A) $2e^{\log 3}$
   B) $\dfrac{\log 3}{2e}$
   C) $\dfrac{1}{2} e^{\log 3}$
   D) $2e^3$
   E) 10^{3e}

107) Solve $3e^{2x} = 1$

   A) $\dfrac{\ln 3}{2}$
   B) $2 \ln 3$
   C) $3 \ln 2$
   D) $\dfrac{\ln 2}{3}$
   E) $\dfrac{\ln \frac{1}{3}}{2}$

108) Solve $\sin^2 x + \cos^2 x + \tan^2 x = 1$ within the domain $[0, 2\pi)$.

    A) $0, \pi, 2\pi$

    B) $0, \pi$

    C) $\dfrac{\pi}{2}, \dfrac{3\pi}{2}$

    D) $0, \dfrac{\pi}{2}, \dfrac{3\pi}{2}$

    E) $0, \dfrac{\pi}{2}, \pi$

109) Solve $1 - \csc^2 2x = 0$ within the domain $[0, 2\pi)$.

    A) $\dfrac{\pi}{2}, \dfrac{\pi}{4}, 2\pi$

    B) $0, \dfrac{\pi}{2}, \pi$

    C) $\dfrac{\pi}{4}, \dfrac{3\pi}{4}$

    D) $\dfrac{\pi}{2}, \pi, 2\pi$

    E) $\dfrac{\pi}{2}, \dfrac{2\pi}{3}$

110) Solve $x^2 + 13x = 2$

    A) $\dfrac{169 \pm \sqrt{171}}{8}$

    B) $\dfrac{-1 \pm \sqrt{105}}{26}$

    C) $78, 91$

    D) $\dfrac{-169 \pm \sqrt{177}}{2}$

    E) None of the above

Functions: Concept, Properties and Operations

(7 Questions)

111) What is the domain of the following equation?

$$y = \frac{2x}{x\sqrt{12-x}}$$

A) $x \neq 0, x < 12$
B) $x \neq 0, x \leq 12$
C) $x > 12$
D) $x \leq 0, x \geq 12$
E) All real numbers

112) What is the range of the function graphed below?

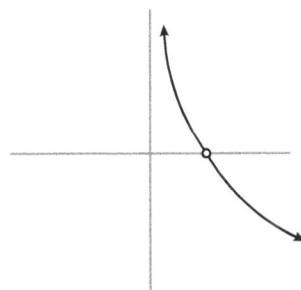

A) $[-\infty, 0] \cup [0, \infty]$
B) $[-\infty, 0) \cup (0, \infty]$
C) $(-\infty, 0) \cup (0, \infty)$
D) $(0, \infty]$
E) All real numbers

113) Factor $a^2b^2 + 2ab + 1$

A) $(ab+b)(ab+1)$
B) $(a+ab)(a+ab)$
C) $(a^2+b)(1+b)$
D) $(ab+1)^2$
E) $(a+bc)(1+a)$

114) Factor $a^2x^2 - y^2$

　　A) $(ax+1)^2$
　　B) $(ax+y)(ax-y)$
　　C) $(ax+1)(ay+x)$
　　D) $(ax+y)(x+y)$
　　E) $(ax+y)(x+ay)$

115) What is the domain of the quadratic equation?

　　A) $a > 0$, $4ac > b^2$
　　B) $4ac > b^2$
　　C) $a > 0$
　　D) $4ac > b^2$, $a \neq 0$
　　E) The quadratic equation has no domain

116) If $f(x) = 3x+1$ and $g(x) = x^2$, what is $g(f(g(x)))$

　　A) $3(3x^4 + 2x^2 + 1)$
　　B) $3x^4 + 6x^2 + 1$
　　C) $9x^4 + 6x^2 + 1$
　　D) $3x^2 + 1$
　　E) $9x^2 + 6x + 1$

117) Determine the inverse of $y = \dfrac{x+7}{2x}$.

　　A) $y = \dfrac{2x-1}{7}$
　　B) $y = \dfrac{7}{2x-1}$
　　C) $y = \dfrac{7}{2x+1}$
　　D) $y = \dfrac{2x+1}{7}$
　　E) Cannot be determined

118) If $f(x) = x^2 + 17$, then $f^{-1}(x) = ?$

    A) $\sqrt{x-17}$

    B) $\sqrt{x+17}$

    C) $\sqrt{x^2+17}$

    D) $\sqrt{x^2-17}$

    E) $\sqrt{x}-17x^2$

Representations of Functions: Symbolic, Graphical and Tabular

(15 Questions)

119) The function $y = 3^x + 1$ models which type of equation?

    A) Quadratic

    B) Exponential

    C) Logarithmic

    D) Third degree polynomial

    E) Piecewise defined

120) The graph shown below displays which type of function?

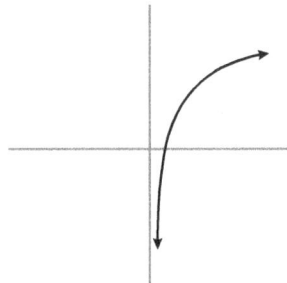

    A) Exponential

    B) Linear

    C) Radical

    D) Logarithmic

    E) Piecewise

121) The table below most likely represents data taken from which type of equation?

x	y
1	2
2	4
3	8
4	16
5	32
6	64
7	128
8	256

A) Exponential
B) Linear
C) Quadratic
D) Logarithmic
E) Piecewise

122) Which of the following is the correct graph of $\log(x+1)$

A)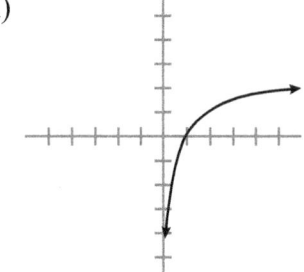

C)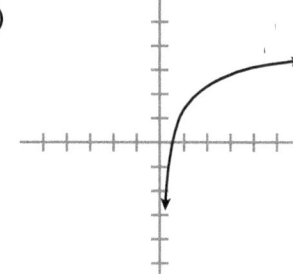

B)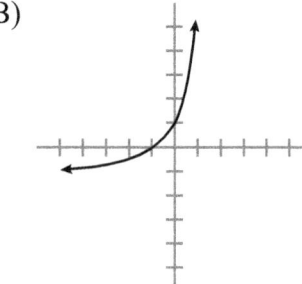

D)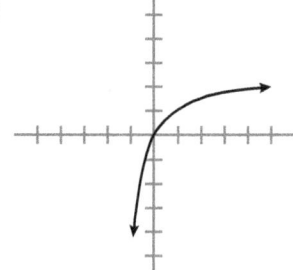

E) None of the above

123) The graph below most likely belongs to which of the following equations?

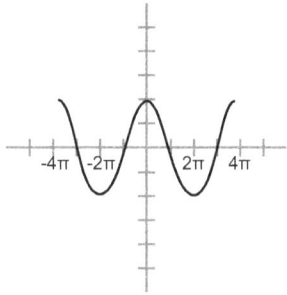

A) $\dfrac{1}{2}\cos(2x)$

B) $2\sin\left(\dfrac{1}{2}x\right)$

C) $2\cos\left(\dfrac{1}{2}x\right)$

D) $\dfrac{1}{2}\sin(2x)$

E) $-2\cos\left(\dfrac{1}{2}x\right)$

124) The graph below demonstrates which type of equation?

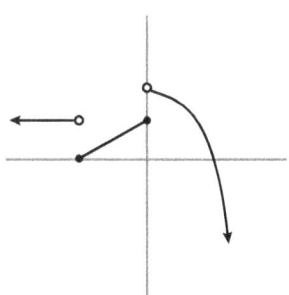

A) Linear
B) Quadratic
C) Exponential
D) Logarithmic
E) Piecewise

125) The equation below represents which of the following graphs?

$$y = \begin{cases} \dfrac{-3}{2}x - \dfrac{3}{2}, \text{ if } x \leq 1 \\ 2, \text{ if } -1 < x < 1 \\ (x-1)^2 + 1, \text{ if } x \geq 1 \end{cases}$$

A)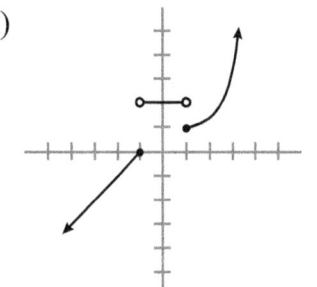

C)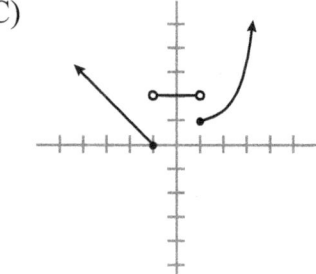

B)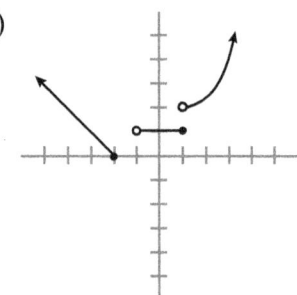

D)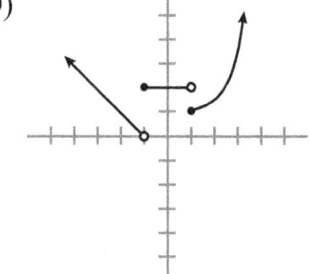

E) None of the above

126) Which of the following is the correct graph of $y = |x-1| + 3$?

A)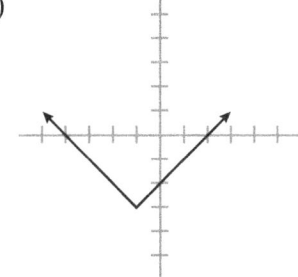

C)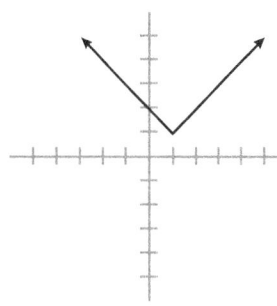

B)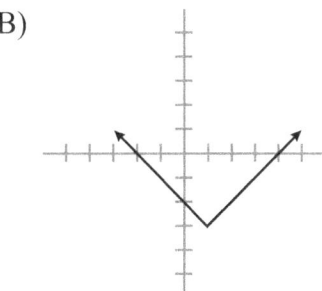

D)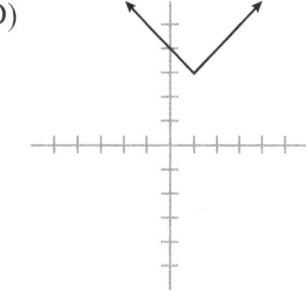

E) None of the above

127) Which of the following is the correct graph of $y = \sqrt{x+1} - \frac{1}{2}$?

A)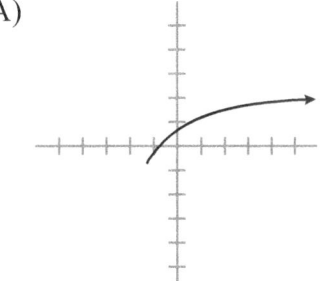

C)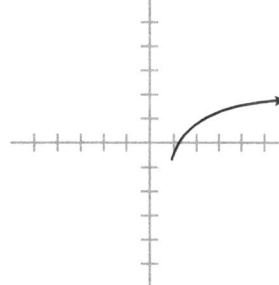

B)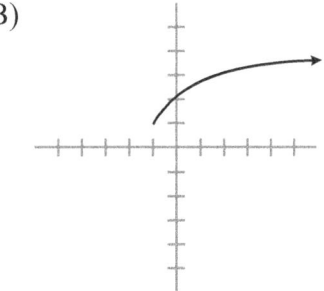

D)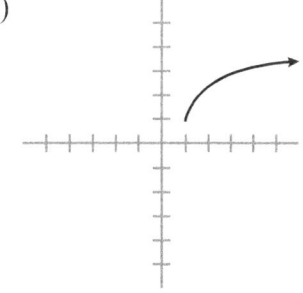

E) None of the above

128) Which of the following is NOT a polynomial graph?

A)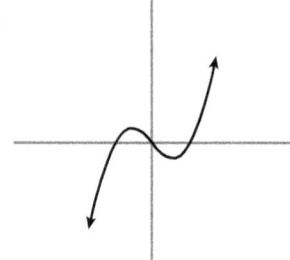

C)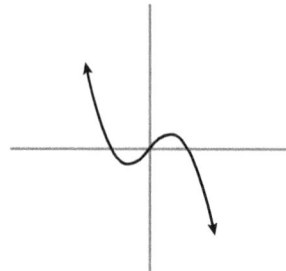

B)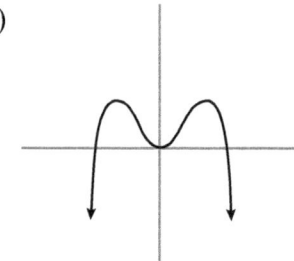

D)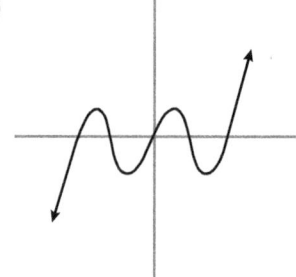

E) All of the above are polynomial graphs

129) Which of the following graphs has domain and range of all real numbers?

A)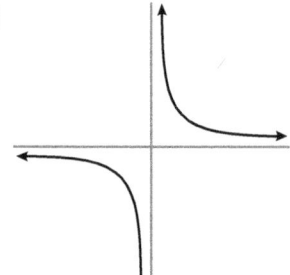

C)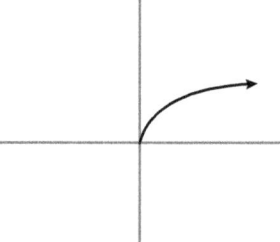

B)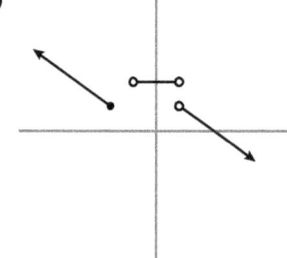

D)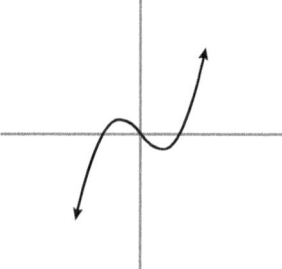

E) None of the above

130) Which of the following is the graph of $y = -2\csc bx$?

A)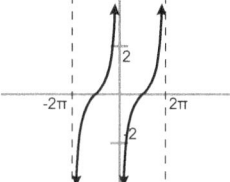

C)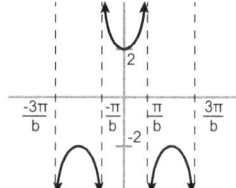

B)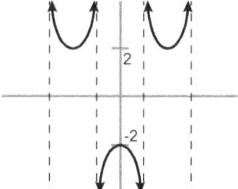

D)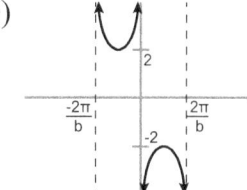

E) None of the above

131) Which of the following is the graph of $y = -2\sec bx$?

A)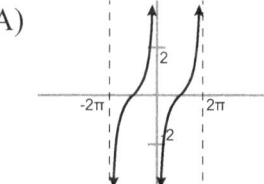

C)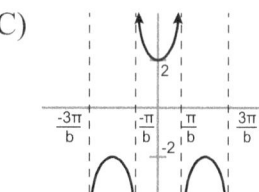

B)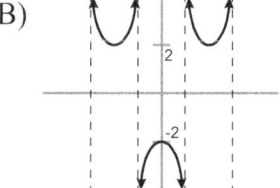

D)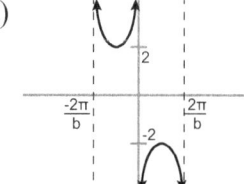

E) None of the above

132) Which of the following describes the difference between the graphs of $y = \sqrt{x}$ and $y = -\sqrt{x+3}$?

   A) The second equation is the same as the first, but reflected across the x-axis and shifted three to the left.
   B) The second equation is the same as the first, but reflected across the y-axis and shifted three to the left.
   C) The second equation is the same as the first, but reflected across the x-axis and shifted three to the right.
   D) The second equation is the same as the first, but reflected across the y-axis and shifted three to the right.
   E) The second equation is the same as the first.

133) Which of the following best describes the difference between the graphs of $\frac{x^2}{16} + \frac{y^2}{4} = 1$ and $x^2 + y^2 = 25$?

   A) The two equations are both circles, but the first has a much smaller radius.
   B) The first equation is that of an ellipse, and the second equation is that of a circle.
   C) The two equations are both ellipses, but the second is more circular than the first.
   D) The first equation is that of a circle, and the second equation is that of an ellipse.
   E) The two equations are both ellipses, but the first is more circular than the second.

Analytic Geometry

(5 Questions)

134) Which of the following graphs represents the equation $(y+2)^2 + x^2 = 4$

A)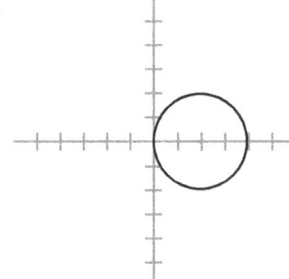

E)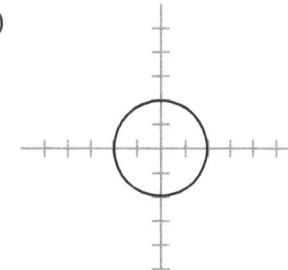

B)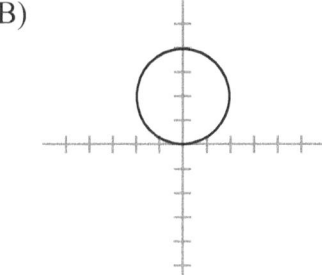

D)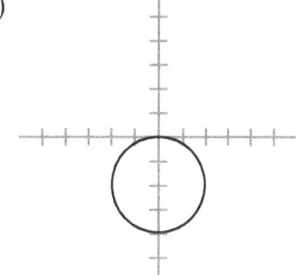

C)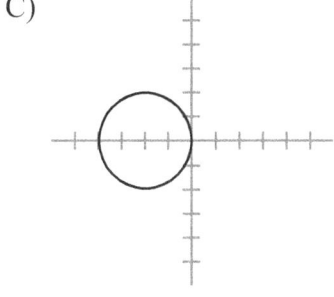

135) Which of the following correctly states a pair of equal distances as labeled on the parabola below?

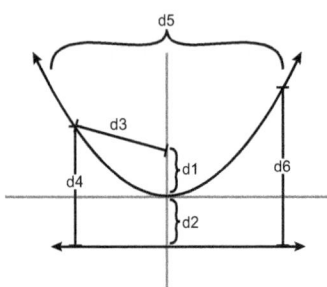

A) d1 and d2
B) d5 and d6
C) d2 and d3
D) d3 and d4
E) Both A and D

136) Which of the following is a hyperbola?

A)

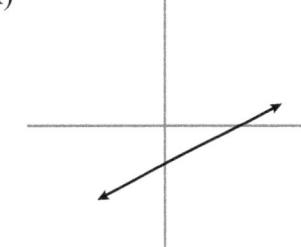

B)

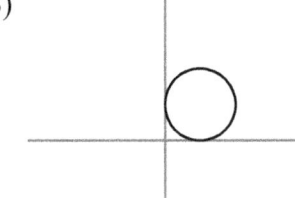

C)

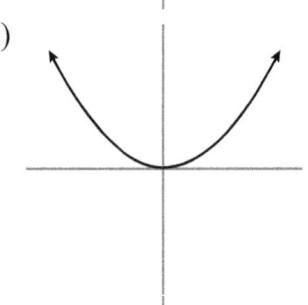

D)

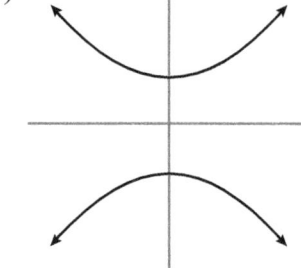

E)

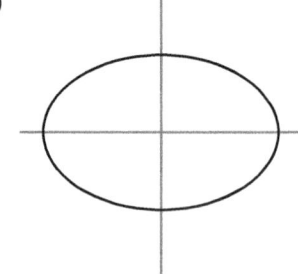

137) Which of the following is NOT an ellipse?

A)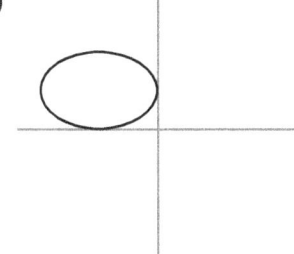

B)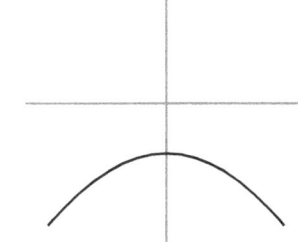

C)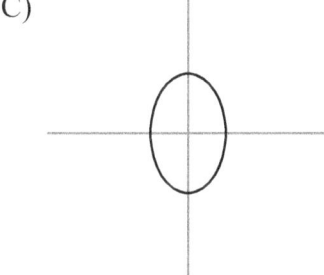

D)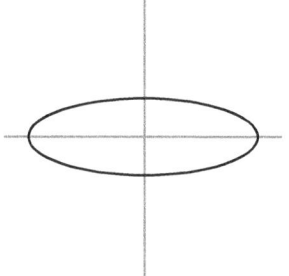

E) All of the above are ellipses

138) Which of the following is a parabola?

A)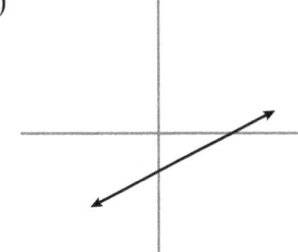

D)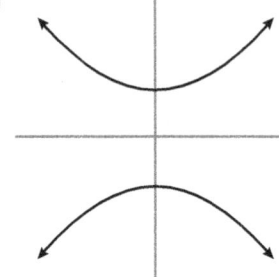

B)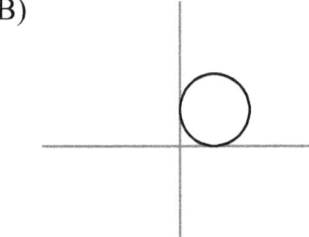

E)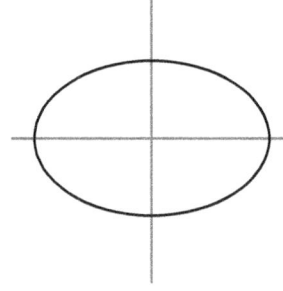

C)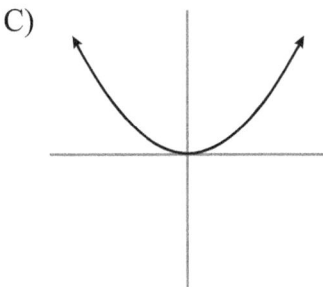

Trigonometry and Its Applications

(7 Questions)

139) $\sin^2 x + \cos^2 x + \dfrac{1-\cos(2x)}{1+\cos(2x)}$ simplifies to which of the following?

A) $1+\cot^2 2x$

B) $1-\csc x$

C) $\tan^2 2x$

D) $\sec^2 x$

E) 1

140) Evaluate $y = \frac{1}{2}\cos x + \pi$ for the corresponding radian values of 30, 60 and 90 degrees respectively.

A) $\frac{1+4\pi}{4}, \frac{4\pi+\sqrt{3}}{4}, \pi$

B) $\frac{4\pi+\sqrt{3}}{4}, \frac{1+4\pi}{4}, \pi$

C) $\frac{1+4\pi}{4}, \frac{4\pi+\sqrt{3}}{4}, 1+\pi$

D) $\frac{4\pi+\sqrt{3}}{4}, \frac{1+4\pi}{4}, 1+\pi$

E) $\frac{2\pi+\sqrt{3}}{2}, \frac{1+2\pi}{2}, \pi$

141) A person is trying to determine how tall a building is. They know that the shadow it casts is 15 feet long across the ground at 6 o'clock when they measure it. They determine that the angle the shadow comes off the building is 60 degrees. Approximately how tall is the building?

A) 15 ft
B) 17 ft
C) 19 ft
D) 21 ft
E) 23 ft

142) If $f(x) = \cos(x)$ and $g(x) = \arccos(3x+1)$, what is $f(g(x))$?

A) cos(x)
B) sin(3x+1)
C) 3x+1
D) 0
E) Cannot be determined

143) $\cos^{-1}\left(-\dfrac{1}{2}\right) = ?$

   A) $\dfrac{2\pi}{3}$

   B) $-\dfrac{\pi}{3}$

   C) $\dfrac{\pi}{6}$

   D) $-\dfrac{2\pi}{6}$

   E) Cannot be determined without more information

144) Determine what angle the sun must be hitting a $9\sqrt{3}$ foot tall tree at to make it cast a nine foot shadow.

   A) $\dfrac{\pi}{6}$

   B) $-\dfrac{\pi}{3}$

   C) $-\dfrac{2\pi}{6}$

   D) $\dfrac{2\pi}{3}$

   E) $\dfrac{\pi}{2}$

145) Which of the following is the graph of $2\sin(x)+1$?

A)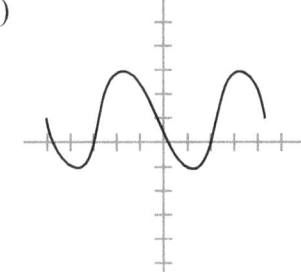

C)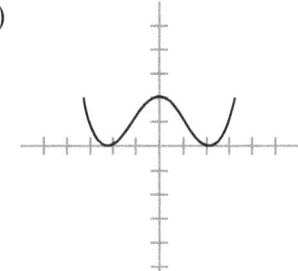

B)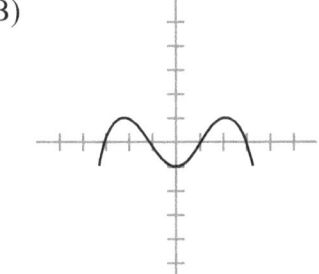

D)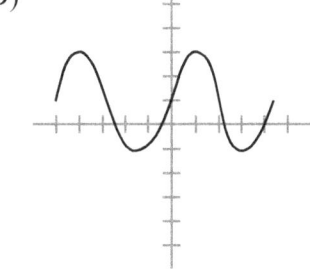

E)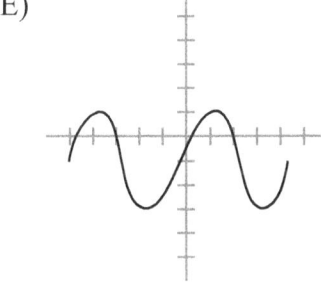

Functions as Models

(5 Questions)

146) A company is trying to create a function to model their total profit (*p*). They know that they must pay 200 dollars to buy the equipment they need to make the product. From there, they determine that they must spend 30 cents for every product that they make (*x*), as long as they make less than 1,000. If they make 1,000 or more then the cost drops to 20 cents each. From selling the products, they make the amount they spent to make a product times the square of the number of products produced. Which of the following equations correctly models their profit?

  A) $p = .3x^2 - .3x + 200$
  B) $p = .3x^2 - .3x + .2x^2 - .2x + 200$
  C) $p = .3x^2 - 200x + .3x$
  D) $p = .3(.2x^2) - 200$
  E) $p = \begin{cases} 200 - .3x + .3x^2, \text{ if } x < 1,000 \\ 200 - .2x + .2x^2, \text{ if } x \geq 1,000 \end{cases}$

147) A car is accelerating along a straight road. The table below gives its position (*x*) at various times (*t*). Based on the information provided on the table, the cars position (during the time period provided) would most correctly be modeled using what type of function?

t	x
2	14
4	26
6	45
8	73
10	112

  A) Quadratic
  B) A fifth degree polynomial
  C) Logarithmic
  D) Exponential
  E) Linear

148) A person is biking at a constant speed down the road, but has to come to a complete stop when they come to a busy intersection. When they are allowed to go they once again return to a steady pace. Which of the following graphs best models their position throughout the time period?

A)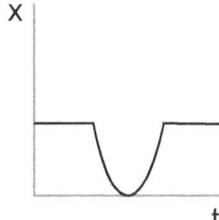

C)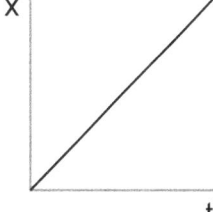

B)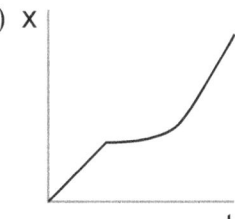

D)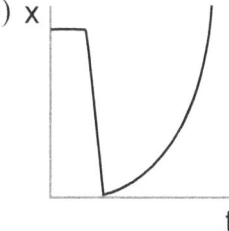

E)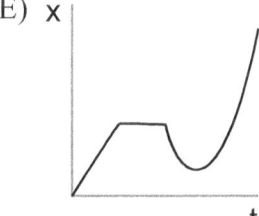

149) A scientist it attempting to model the population growth of a certain species of plant over time (t). He knows that the population grows at an exponential rate of base 2 over time (measured in months). However, as the population grows, a number of plants also die. Every month 12 plants die. Which of the following equations correctly models the growth of the population (p) of plants?

A) $p = 12(t-1)^t$
B) $p = 12t - 2^t$
C) $p = 2t - 12^t$
D) $p = 2^t - 12t$
E) $p = 12 - x^2 + e$

150) A person hires a company to place new carpet in their home. They will remove the old carpet themselves, so there will be no charge for that. They can't decide if they want to put new carpet in just a few rooms (r), or if they want to redo the whole house (which includes 12 carpeted rooms). They are shown the following formula which describes the cost (C) of putting in new carpet.

$$C = \begin{cases} 10r^2 + 500r, \text{ if } r \leq 5 \\ 10r^2 + 400r, \text{ if } 5 < r < 10 \\ 10r^2 + 300r, \text{ if } r \geq 10 \end{cases}$$

Which of the following correctly interprets the formula?

A) The least amount of money that they could spend would be to do one room for $510, but to do their whole house it would cost them $5,040.
B) It would only cost them ten dollars more to do six rooms than it would to do five rooms.
C) There will be a per room rate of $10r^2$ no matter how many rooms they do, but the additional per room price after that will decrease the more rooms that they do.
D) Based on the formula, the size of the room doesn't actually affect the cost of carpeting it.
E) All of the above statements are correct.

Answer Key

#	Ans	#	Ans	#	Ans	#	Ans
1.	B	40.	C	79.	A	118.	A
2.	A	41.	C	80.	A	119.	B
3.	B	42.	D	81.	D	120.	D
4.	C	43.	C	82.	C	121.	A
5.	C	44.	A	83.	D	122.	D
6.	C	45.	D	84.	A	123.	C
7.	A	46.	D	85.	A	124.	E
8.	C	47.	A	86.	C	125.	C
9.	C	48.	D	87.	B	126.	D
10.	A	49.	D	88.	D	127.	E
11.	D	50.	B	89.	C	128.	E
12.	B	51.	C	90.	C	129.	D
13.	D	52.	B	91.	B	130.	D
14.	A	53.	A	92.	A	131.	B
15.	B	54.	D	93.	A	132.	A
16.	B	55.	A	94.	C	133.	B
17.	A	56.	C	95.	B	134.	D
18.	B	57.	D	96.	A	135.	E
19.	A	58.	B	97.	C	136.	D
20.	A	59.	B	98.	B	137.	B
21.	A	60.	D	99.	D	138.	C
22.	D	61.	B	100.	A	139.	B
23.	B	62.	C	101	C	140.	B
24.	D	63.	B	102.	E	141.	C
25.	B	64.	D	103.	E	142.	C
26.	B	65.	A	104.	C	143.	A
27.	A	66.	A	105.	D	144.	D
28.	B	67.	C	106.	A	145.	D
29.	A	68.	C	107.	E	146.	E
30.	A	69.	A	108.	B	147.	B
31.	C	70.	D	109.	C	148.	B
32.	A	71.	A	110.	E	149.	D
33.	B	72.	B	111.	A	150.	E
34.	C	73.	A	112.	C		
35.	B	74.	C	113.	D		
36.	D	75.	C	114.	B		
37.	A	76.	A	115.	E		
38.	A	77.	C	116.	C		
39.	B	78.	B	117.	B		

Special Information for the CLEP Test

The Precalculus test is a total of 48 questions. In the first section of the test, there are 25 questions which must be answered in 50 minutes or less. The second section will require you to answer 23 questions in 40 minutes. No calculator is allowed for the second section.

The CLEP Precalculus test is administered via a computer terminal at an accredited institution. A graphing calculator will be available on the computer. It is available during all questions of section 1. However, only **some** of the questions require the use of the calculator. You should be able to know when and how to use it. Students must be familiar with the calculator which can be downloaded for a free 30 day trial at www.collegeboard.org/CLEP/Precalculus.

Test Taking Strategies

Here are some test-taking strategies that are specific to this test and to other CLEP tests in general:
- Keep your eyes on the time. Pay attention to how much time you have left.
- Read the entire question and read all the answers. Many questions are not as hard to answer as they may seem. Sometimes, a difficult sounding question really only is asking you how to read an accompanying chart. Chart and graph questions are on most CLEP tests and should be an easy free point.
- If you don't know the answer immediately, the new computer-based testing lets you mark questions and come back to them later if you have time.
- Read the wording carefully. Some words can give you hints to the right answer. There are no exceptions to an answer when there are words in the question such as always, all or none. If one of the answer choices includes most or some of the right answers, but not all, then that is not the correct answer. Here is an example:

The primary colors include all of the following:

A) Red, Yellow, Blue, Green
B) Red, Green, Yellow
C) Red, Orange, Yellow
D) Red, Yellow, Blue
E) None of the above

Although item A includes all the right answers, it also includes an incorrect answer, making it incorrect. If you didn't read it carefully, were in a hurry, or didn't know the material well, you might fall for this.
- Make a guess on a question that you do not know the answer to. There is no penalty for an incorrect answer. Eliminate the answer choices that you know are incorrect. For example, this will let your guess be a 1 in 3 chance instead.

What Your Score Means

Based on your score, you may, or may not, qualify for credit at your specific institution. At University of Phoenix, a score of 50 is passing for full credit. At Utah Valley University, the score is unpublished, the school will accept credit on a case-by-case basis. Another school, Brigham Young University (BYU) does not accept CLEP credit. To find out what score you need for credit, you need to get that information from your school's website or academic advisor.

You can score between 20 and 80 on any CLEP test. Some exams include percentile ranks. Each correct answer is worth one point. You lose no points for unanswered or incorrect questions.

Test Preparation

How much you need to study depends on your knowledge of a subject area. If you are interested in literature, took it in school, or enjoy reading then your studying and preparation for the literature or humanities test will not need to be as intensive as someone who is new to literature.

This book is much different than the regular CLEP study guides. This book actually teaches you the information that you need to know to pass the test. If you are particularly interested in an area, or you want more information, do a quick search online. We've tried not to include too much depth in areas that are not as essential on the test. Everything in this book will be on the test. It is important to understand all major theories and concepts listed in the table of contents. It is also very important to know any bolded words.

Don't worry if you do not understand or know a lot about the area. With minimal study, you can complete and pass the test.

One of the fallacies of other test books is test questions. People assume that the **content of the questions are similar to what will be on the test. That is not the case.** They are only to test your "test taking skills" so for those who know to read a question carefully, there is not much added value from taking a "fake" test.

To prepare for the test, make a series of goals. Allot a certain amount of time to review the information you have already studied and to learn additional material. Take notes as you study, as it will help you learn the material.

Legal Note

All rights reserved. This Study Guide, Book and Flashcards are protected under US Copyright Law. No part of this book or study guide or flashcards may be reproduced, distributed or stored in a retrieval system, or transmitted in any form or by any means, electronic, mechanical, photocopying, recording, or otherwise, without the prior written permission of the publisher Breely Crush Publishing, LLC. This manual is not supported by or affiliated with the College Board, creators of the CLEP test. CLEP is a registered trademark of the College Entrance Examination Board, which does not endorse this book.

FLASHCARDS

This section contains flashcards for you to use to further your understanding of the material and test yourself on important concepts, names or dates. Read the term or question then flip the page over to check the answer on the back. Keep in mind that this information may not be covered in the text of the study guide. Take your time to study the flashcards, you will need to know and understand these concepts to pass the test.

Terms	**Algebraic expression**
Ellipse	**Hyperbola**
Like or unlike terms? 14, -14	**Like or unlike terms?** 3x2, 3x
Coefficient of the variable	**Polynomial**

Collection of terms that are separated by arithmetic operations	Numbers and variables
Look like two parabolas that are reflected over a line of symmetry	Locus of all points in a plane such as the sum of the distances between two fixed points
Unlike	Like
Expression containing the sum of a finite number of terms	The number multiplied by the variable

FOIL	Factor
Simplify	Algebraic equation
Balance in equations	Quadratic equation
What is the solution to a quadratic equation?	Vertex

Two numbers or terms that when multiplied together yield the original term	First, out, inner, last
Must contain an equal sign	Solve or reduce
One variable is an equation that can be changed into the form $ax^2+bx+c=0$	The value of each side of the equation is the same
The lowest point on the parabola	The root of the polynomial $ax^2+bx+c=0$

In graphing the term x runs horizontal or vertical?

In graphing the term y runs horizontal or vertical?

What is absolute value?

| |

≠

≤

≥

<

Vertical	Horizontal
Notation for absolute value	The distance between a number and 0 on the number line
Notation for less than or equal to	Notation for not equal to
Notation for less than	Notation for greater than or equal to

>

Parallel lines

Perpendicular lines

⊥

| |

Logarithms

Natural logarithms

When are logarithms and exponents used?

Two lines are parallel if they lie on the same plane and never intersect	Notation for greater than
Notation for perpendicular	Two lines are perpendicular if their intersection forms a right angle
The exponent of a positive number	Notation for parallel
To calculate simple & compound interest and exponential growth	Have a base "e" which is a constant

Radius	Diameter
Chord	Central Angle
Arc	Major arc
{ }	Another name for empty set

Diameter of a circle is twice the radius	A line segment joining the center to a point on the circle
Formed by two radii	A line that goes through the center of the circle
An arc that is greater than a semicircle	Continuous part of the circle
Null Set	Empty Set

NOTES

NOTES

NOTES

NOTES

NOTES

NOTES

NOTES

NOTES

NOTES

NOTES

NOTES

NOTES

NOTES

NOTES